CHRIS SIDWELLS

cycling
for fitness

Get fast, get fit
in seven weeks

DK

LONDON, NEW YORK, MELBOURNE, MUNICH, and DELHI

To everyone and anyone trying to improve their fitness

Project Editor **Nasim Mawji**
Project Art Editor **Miranda Harvey**
Senior Art Editor **Anne Fisher**
Managing Editor **Penny Warren**
Managing Art Editor **Marianne Markham**
Publishing Director **Mary-Clare Jerram**
DTP Designer **Sonia Charbonnier**
Production Controller **Sarah Sherlock**
Photographer **Russell Sadur**

First American edition 2006
05 06 07 08 09 10 9 8 7 6 5 4 3 2 1

Published in the United States by
DK Publishing, Inc.
375 Hudson Street
New York, New York 10014

DK Books are available at special discounts for bulk purchases
for sales promotions, premiums, fund-raising, or educational use.
For details, contact: DK Publishing Special Markets,
375 Hudson Street, New York, New York 10014 or
SpecialSales@dk.com

Cataloging-in-Publication data is available from
the Library of Congress
ISBN 0 7566 1739 1

Color reproduction by Colourscan, Singapore
Printed and bound by Star Standard, Singapore

Discover more at
www.dk.com

CONTENTS

GETTING STARTED

Cycling is great exercise, but it has so much more to offer you. It is a pastime you can take up regardless of your age or current state of fitness, and it can help you to lose weight, tone your muscles, and strengthen your heart and lungs. You'll be working out, whether you explore locally or ride further afield. On top of this, it's fun. It's a great way to rediscover the freedom that many of us first enjoyed as children, as the world whizzed past us on our bikes. Bikes are more sophisticated these days, but the fun's still there. In these days of gridlock traffic, riding your bike to work is a money-saving, healthy, and quick alternative to cars and public transport. Get started and rediscover the simple thrill of riding your bicycle outside.

WHY CYCLE?

There is nothing quite like cycling: The thrill of speed, the feeling of traveling along under your own power, the breeze in your face, the sounds, the fresh air. I enjoy the sensation of muscles tightening as you work to climb a hill, the feeling of achievement when you reach the top, the view, and the swooping freewheel down the other side. Cycling is freedom, fun, travel and exercise rolled into one.

Environmentally friendly

In today's developed society, our dependence on cars threatens not only our health for easing us into lives of physical inactivity but also the environment. When you consider that the average car takes up the same area on the road as at least five bicycles, the effect of more people cycling on daily commutes to work, to see friends, or to visit a store is obvious. In 2000 in Boston, MA, for example, roughly 16,000 people cycled to work. If just ten percent more were added to this number, an area equivalent to 8,000 cars would be freed up. That would ease congestion,

Go by bike
Help the environment and your health: swap your bike for just a few of the journeys that you would normally make by car.

reduce noxious, environmentally damaging emissions, and decrease travel time for everyone.

In the US more cycle paths are being created in cities in order to encourage cyclists onto the roads. In 2005, the latest Transportation Bill guarantees a minimum of $3 billion will be spent on cycling programs through 2009.

Low cost and practical

Bikes are convenient. Not only do they require very little maintenance and hardly any running costs, it takes minimal space to store them. You don't have to pay parking fees or fines for them, and you don't have to put gas in them. In fact, if you were to give up your car entirely, you could save an estimated $5,000 per year in payments, insurance, and maintenance costs.

Bikes are adaptable, too. The same bike that you ride to work can take you into the countryside, or go on a trip. Regardless of the setting, riding it will be getting you fitter. What else can act as exercise machine, transport, and a vehicle for adventure?

No form of fitness training brings consistent results over a broader range of ages and backgrounds than cycling. You can train when and where you want, with minimal specialized clothing and equipment. With few technical points to master, in no time at all you'll feel accomplished and able to go places and see things on your bike.

Explore the great outdoors
A bike can serve as a convenient and economical mode of transport in a city, but it can also be your means of escape.

arm muscles
riding out of the saddle or
on off-road terrain tones and
strengthens the muscles in
your upper and lower arms

shoulder and chest muscles
gripping the handlebars to
control the bike strengthens
and tones the chest and
shoulder muscles

core muscles
balancing on a bike activates
the muscles in your lower
back and abdomen and
helps to strengthen them

hip and leg joints
the bike supports your
weight so no strain is
put on your hip, knee,
or ankle joints

resistance training
changing gears alters
the level of resistance
that your muscles work
against, so you can
control the intensity
of your workout

heart and lungs
the lungs work hard
to bring oxygen into
the body while the heart
pumps furiously to distribute
it to the muscles

leg muscles
pedaling tones and
strengthens the
muscles in the thighs
and calves, as they
work hard to power
the effort

Why cycle for fitness?

Cycling is one of the few exercises that can provide a good aerobic, or cardiovascular, workout at the same time as toning and strengthening your muscles. It is a low-impact exercise—the bike supports the weight of your body—so your joints are protected and are not put under strain. And because you can change gears and choose your terrain, cycling offers you a lot of control over the intensity of your workout. Although the muscles in your legs work hard to power the pedaling action, cycling will strengthen, shape, and tone your entire body.

Building aerobic fitness

Cycling, even at a steady pace, raises your heart rate. Your heart and lungs have to work hard to supply oxygen to the muscles so that they can power the effort of pedaling. The more aerobic, or "cardio", training that you do, the fitter you become and the more efficient your body becomes at supplying your muscles with oxygen.

The benefits of a good level of aerobic fitness are far reaching. You will find that you are better able to cope with the physical demands of your daily life, but you will also notice that you are more alert and can concentrate more easily. You will sleep better and, as a result, you will look and feel better about yourself. Regular aerobic exercise, combined with a healthy, balanced diet, can help you control your weight, reduce body fat, strengthen your heart and blood vessels, improve circulation, and even lower blood pressure.

Developing muscular fitness

A popular misconception about cycling is that it only works the muscles of the legs. The action of pedaling does strengthen and tone the muscles in the calves and thighs, but other muscles in the torso and arms must work hard too. The position of your body on the bike as you pedal provides a platform for you to work against, and activates the "core" muscles in your torso. These are the muscles that support your spine, keep your lower back strong, and promote good posture. When you ride out of the saddle, you target the muscles in your upper body—those in the arms, shoulders, and chest. When you cycle hard and increase your speed, you push hard with your legs as you pull up on the handlebars and cycling becomes a full-body muscular workout.

Slow- and fast-twitch muscle fibers

Muscles consist of two types of muscle fibers: Slow-twitch and fast-twitch. Nearly every muscle in our bodies is made up of a genetically determined proportion of the two. Slow-twitch muscle fibers are more abundant, and they power steady, constant efforts such as low- to medium-intensity cycling, running, or walking. Fast-twitch muscle fibers power high-intensity bursts of effort that can only be sustained for short periods of time, such as sprinting or lifting a heavy weight. Fast-twitch fibers are thicker than slow-twitch ones, so targeting them can help to give muscle more shape and definition. Cycling will tone muscles, but because it is balanced with aerobic work, it won't build bulky muscle.

One of the advantages of cycling over other forms of exercise is the control that it gives you over the type and intensity of your workout. By using the variable gears on a bike, or by riding up a hill or sprinting, you target fast-twitch muscle fibers as part of an overall training program, without the need for any additional specialist equipment. Stimulating the maximum number of fast-twitch muscle fibers during a cycling session has one further benefit: It raises your metabolic rate, so you increase the number of calories that you burn, even when you are not exercising.

Something for everyone

Cycling is an excellent form of exercise for all ages and fitness levels. Because the bike carries the rider's weight, children can cycle with no danger of stress being placed on their growing bones, while older people can enjoy cycling without the risk of damaging their joints. Anyone who is overweight will find 20 minutes of cycling more enjoyable than high-impact, weight-bearing workouts such as jogging or aerobics, and those with a history of injury can also benefit from a cycling program.

Because it is so easy to control the intensity of your workout, you can raise your heart rate without putting your body under too much duress. Even those who already have a good level of fitness will find that they can cycle for longer than with many other activities.

Convenience and flexibility

Part of the appeal of cycling is its convenience. You can ride indoors or outside, and on- or off-road. The minute that you set off from your doorstep, you can begin training. If you decide to cycle to work, you can be improving your fitness at the very same time as you commute. Another attraction

Fun for all the family
Children like cycling because it is fast and exciting; many find it a more interesting alternative to traditional school sports.

is that it doesn't require specialist skills. The techniques are easy to master—most people already know how to cycle because they learned to do it as children. On top of this, modern bikes are easy to ride. Even entry-level bikes will have plenty of gears, good tires, and weigh very little.

Cycling is also the perfect exercise for families and groups of friends to do together. It is great fun. You can travel to different places on your bike rides, and see things that those in cars won't. You can easily integrate family rides into the program outlined in this book. Even if you have to slow your pace so that everyone can keep up, you will still be getting a good workout if you carry a child in a child's seat, for example, or the ingredients for a family picnic in your backpack. Alternatively, you can cycle alone. A ride can be a solitary, contemplative experience, and your bike a means of escape.

Whatever type of cycling you decide on, if you do it regularly and in conjunction with a healthy lifestyle, it will improve your fitness level. Cycling is also a good way to keep fit for other sports, or as part of a cross-training program where you use several activities to keep fit. Many marathon runners, walkers, dancers, and swimmers use cycling as part of their training.

Starting out

If you are starting from a low level of fitness, have a history of injuries, or haven't ridden a bike for a while, take it slowly to begin with. Do some general, easy riding before embarking on the seven-week program featured in this book. Start with short, 15-minute rides, on flat roads or trails, and slowly build up the duration of your outings.

It's easy to fit cycling into your life. Where you might have driven, or gone by bus, train, or on foot, go by bike instead. It will take no time at all for you to build up confidence. Some YMCAs and other community organizations offer short courses on

THE BENEFITS OF CYCLING

You will feel the benefits of regular cycling on both physical and mental levels. Listed below are just some of the many benefits that cycling has to offer:

- burns calories, so it is an excellent form of exercise for weight-loss and control
- provides you with both a cardiovascular and a resistance workout at the same time
- shapes and tones the muscles of your entire body
- improves circulation and strengthens your heart; in some cases, it can lower blood pressure
- minimizes strain on joints and bones because the bike carries the rider's weight
- increases energy levels
- lifts mood
- boosts your body's immune system
- gives a healthy appearance to skin and hair
- improves confidence and self-esteem
- improves quality of life, because as fitness levels increase everyday activities such as climbing stairs become easier
- encourages better sleep
- strengthens core muscles in the back and abdomen, which helps prevent lower back problems and encourage good posture
- creates feelings of happiness and contentment because it causes endorphins to be released into your blood
- improves ability to concentrate
- reduces anxiety levels

cycling safety and skills. If you feel nervous about riding on roads, look for parks and special cyclists' trails. Check with the YMCA or your local bike shop for their locations. Don't let anything get in the way of riding your bike; you stand to gain so much and can have so much fun along the way.

BIKES AND EQUIPMENT

You don't need expensive or sophisticated equipment to begin cycling. In the pages that follow I guide you through the process of choosing and buying a bike that is most suitable for your needs—one that will carry you safely and comfortably over the terrain on which you plan to ride, and one that fits you correctly. Refer to these pages for advice on essential equipment such as helmets, saddles, tires, and lights, and learn exactly what your bike repair kit should hold. Also, this section will help ensure that you are dressed comfortably and correctly for the weather conditions in which you plan to cycle, whether you ride on- or off-road.

BUYING A BIKE

With so many bikes on offer these days, the process of choosing and buying one can be daunting. Broadly speaking, bikes fall into three main categories: Road bikes, mountain bikes, and hybrid bikes. Although there are variations within these categories, a good starting point is to consider the type of cycling that you want to do. Bikes are fairly adaptable machines, but each type has its limitations.

What type of bike?

Think for a minute about the type of cycling that you enjoy. Do you like the sensation of traveling at speed? Are there quiet but well-surfaced roads where you plan to cycle? Or will you be going off-road and riding on bumpy terrain?

If you plan to do most of your cycling on roads, you can consider all three types of bike. Road bikes have a similar design to racing bikes. They have dropped handlebars and thin, lightly treaded tires; they are light but still solid and dependable. One consideration is that your riding position on a road bike is quite low and you have to stretch your body to hold the handlebars. You might find this uncomfortable if you are not that supple.

Another option for road riding is the hybrid bike. These can range from road bikes with flat handlebars to bikes that are virtually mountain bikes. Hybrids are perfect for commuting; they have thinner tyres than mountain bikes, allowing good control, and a more upright riding position than a road bike, which enables easy all-round vision in traffic. Hybrids with wider treaded tires are fine for riding off-road, too.

Choose a mountain bike if you plan to do most of your riding off-road. They have good suspension to absorb the jarring effect of bumpy terrain. Mountain bikes are fine on the road, but their heavily treaded tires can slow you down.

CHOOSING A BIKE

With a good idea of how you will use your bike and where you will ride it, you can then begin to consult bike catalogs to get a realistic idea of how much you will need to spend on it.

Then choose your bike shop with care. If a salesperson tries to sell you a bike that is too big or too small, above your budget, or of a different type, find another shop.

Road bike Carbon-fiber forks help cut road vibrations; dropped handlebars enable an aerodynamic body position. Triple chainsets are best for beginners, and if you plan to ride on hilly terrain.

Hybrid bike Choose V-brakes (see *opposite*), and knobbly tires for off-road as well as city riding. Make sure you can sit upright and look behind if you intend to use the bike for commuting.

Mountain bike Buy a bike with a dampened suspension system as they are most effective. There must be 3–4in between your crotch and the top bar when straddling the bike.

WHAT TO LOOK FOR

Correct frame size is essential. Measure your inside leg from crotch to floor, and consult the table (*see right*). Consider some of the key features illustrated below when choosing a bike to suit your needs.

CHOOSING FRAME SIZE

Inside leg measurement	Road frame	Mountain bike frame	S, M, or L
29½–30¾in	48–51cm	14–16in	S
31–32¼in	50–54cm	16–17in	M
32½–34in	53–57cm	17–18in	L
34¼–35½in	56–60cm	19–21in	XL

women should consider a female-specific saddle; ask the bike shop to change it

adjust the seat post up or down to get the correct saddle height

check that you can reach the handlebars comfortably while sitting in the saddle

some hybrids and all road bikes have caliper brakes; other hybrids and all mountain bikes have V, or sometimes disc brakes

there are a wide variety of wheels and tires available; choose according to your needs (*see below*)

triple chainsets fitted to mountain bikes and hybrids have three chainrings for a wide range of gears

WHEELS AND TIRES

Knobbly, wide tires are for off-road riding. Slick, narrow tires on wheels with few spokes are for road riding. Multi-purpose tires are fine for occasional off-roading but are better for roads.

Off-road mountain bike tire Knobbly tread pattern gives the best grip.

Slick road tire Light tread pattern for smoother road riding.

Multi-purpose tire Tread pattern for good grip and smooth riding.

SADDLES

Don't be seduced by an overly padded saddle—it won't be as comfortable as a specially shaped male- or female-specific one that effectively supports your weight.

Male-specific saddle This is long and narrow in shape but supportive.

Female-specific saddle The back of the saddle is slightly broader than the male-specific variety.

SHOES AND PEDALS

Cycling-specific shoes are preferable to other footwear because they support your foot, preventing unnecessary fatigue and strain. They will enhance your cycling performance and ensure comfort. The type of shoe that you choose also depends on whether you use flat pedals, pedals with toe clips, or clipless pedals, and whether you cycle on- or off-road.

Which shoes and pedals?

Pedals are split broadly into three categories. Flat pedals are simply platforms on which you place your feet and push the pedals round. They are effective enough, but they don't allow you to pedal efficiently, since you only use your leg muscles to push down on the pedals, not to pull up. You will not work all the muscles of your legs if you use flat pedals.

The second option is pedals with toe clips. These consist of a plastic or metal clip and a strap that holds your foot in place. They enable you to put slightly more power behind your pedaling than with flat pedals.

The best option is the clipless pedal system, where a cleat attached to the bottom of your shoe clips into the pedal. You cycle most efficiently with this system because you use your leg muscles to push down and also to pull up when you pedal. They also ensure that your foot is always correctly positioned on the pedal. It is easy to click in and then detach your foot from the pedals (*see opposite*). There are clipless road and off-road pedals, and they are compatible with road and off-road shoes. You can use off-road shoes and pedals on the road, especially on a hybrid, and if you commute or walk with your bike. Road shoes are only suitable for road riding, it is difficult to walk in them.

CLIPLESS PEDALS

The workings of road pedals are enclosed within the pedal body, but off-road pedals are open to allow mud to pass through them.

release
tension
adjuster

release
tension
adjuster

Look road pedal Shoes attach to the pedals by means of large cleats, and these pedals can only be used with road shoes; they are not suitable for off-road use, or if you ride a lot in traffic.

Shimano off-road pedal Small cleats attach to both sides of the pedal, so these are ideal if you stop and start often. They are suitable for road use; open design prevents mud from clogging them.

FITTING CLEATS

Positioning the cleats correctly will enable you to transfer maximum leg power into the pedals.

Fitting a cleat to a shoe Put on your cycling shoe and mark it on the outer side where your foot is widest. Draw a line across the sole from the mark to the inside of the shoe, and at right angles to it. Fix the cleat to the shoe so that the line runs through its center and is parallel to it.

TECHNIQUE: CLICKING IN AND OUT

You will benefit most from cycling if you ride with clipless pedals, where you clip a cleat attached to the bottom of your shoe into the pedal. Your foot is attached securely to the pedal, which enables you to apply power at every stage of the pedal revolution. Clipless pedals are safe and very easy to use.

1 Straddle the bike, and support yourself with one foot on the ground. Push the other pedal just past the top of its revolution, and line up the cleat on your shoe with the pedal.

2 Bring the cleat into contact with the pedal, front first, and push down. You will hear and feel a distinct click as the cleat engages. Press down with the engaged foot and lift the other foot off the ground.

3 As the other pedal reaches the top of its revolution, let your foot meet it. Line up the cleat over the pedal, and push down, front of cleat first. Listen and feel for the cleat as it clicks into the pedal.

4 To disengage your shoe from the pedal, simply twist your heel outward. The manufacturer's instructions will tell you how to adjust the tension required to click out of the pedal. Use a low tension to begin with.

EQUIPMENT AND ACCESSORIES

There is such a diverse range of equipment on offer these days that it can often be difficult to differentiate between what is important and what you can do without. Here I outline what I consider to be essential equipment, all of which is fairly inexpensive, that will keep you safe, ensure that your bike is secure, and help to enhance your experience of cycling.

The most important piece of equipment by far is a helmet. These are available from bike shops. Ask a salesperson to help you fit your helmet correctly. In some countries you are required by law to wear one.

You should also always cycle with a spare inner tube, puncture repair kit, and some form of portable inflator such as a mini-pump. Use the spare inner tube to replace a punctured one if you have a flat when out cycling, then repair the old one to use as a spare when you get home. Carrying a spare inner tube may seem overly cautious, but it could save you trying to carry out a repair while shivering at the roadside. Don't be tempted to leave the repair kit behind, since you could be unlucky enough to have two punctures while out on a ride.

An effective lock is essential if you have to leave your bike unattended, especially in an urban area.

Finally, if you ride in the dark, it is essential that you have lights and reflectors. By law you must have a white light at the front of your bike and a red light at the rear. Consider adding reflectors at the front and rear as well as on the pedals. Reflective strips, leg bands, and flashing LED lights are also recommended (*see* Riding at Night, *p.42*).

HELMET

There can be no valid objection to wearing a modern cycling helmet. They are lightweight, they look good, and you are always safer if you ride wearing one. Whether you ride in the city or off-road, a helmet could save your life. It will protect your head and absorb the impact of a crash by crushing and breaking up. Choose a helmet that has been safety tested.

Fitting a helmet The correct size should sit on your head tightly enough to move your scalp when you move the helmet with straps unfastened. Adjust the straps so that the helmet sits straight and level on your head.

side view

ventilation slots help keep your head cool

aerodynamic design reduces wind resistance

inside view

straps can be altered for a better fit

padding ensures a snug, comfortable fit

a removable peak protects the eyes from sun and rain

BASIC EQUIPMENT

You should always cycle with a puncture repair kit and three tire levers, a spare inner tube, and some form of portable inflator such as a mini-pump. You should also carry an Allen wrench multi-tool for undoing bolts. Lights are also essential.

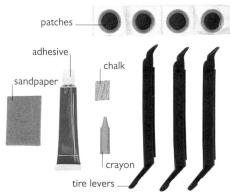

patches
adhesive
chalk
sandpaper
crayon
tire levers

Inner tube Carry a spare to be safe.

Front light You must have a constant white light at the front of your bike.

Puncture repair kit This should consist of a piece of sandpaper, adhesive, chalk, a crayon, and tire levers.

Rear light Attach a red light and red reflector to the rear of your bicycle.

Mini-pump A portable pump such as this one will fit easily in your backpack.

Allen wrench multi-tool This is for undoing Allen bolts (under the saddle, for example).

LOCKS AND SECURITY

Buy the best quality lock you can afford; choose one big enough to wrap the bike and both wheels to a secure object.

Cable lock Use this flexible lock to secure your bike to odd-shaped objects.

U-lock Use this lock to secure your bike to solid posts or railings.

BICYCLE ATTACHMENTS

Bikes often don't come with mudguards, but they can help to keep you clean and dry. Here are some other essential items.

a pannier rack allows you to carry luggage

fit a bottle cage for carrying your water bottle

a mudguard prevents water and mud from spraying you

carry a bottle of water to keep you hydrated

WHAT TO WEAR

Cycling clothing must protect you, and it should also be comfortable. Protect your body's three points of contact with the bike by wearing padded cycling shorts, cycling gloves, and supportive shoes. For comfort, wear layers of clothing, increasing their number in colder weather. All base layers (those closest to your body) should have good "wicking" qualities, or be able to move perspiration away from the skin.

Winter road clothing

Start with a long-sleeved wicking base layer, then add layers according to how cold it is. Several thin layers are more effective than one thick one, because thin layers trap warm air between them.

Bib tights with padded seats are excellent. Most styles cover the bottom half of your torso as well as your legs. Straps that go over your shoulders hold the tights in place and also insulate your lower back.

wear a thermal headband under your helmet to protect your ears

outer layer provides protection from wind and rain

thermal gloves keep hands warm

bib tights keep the legs, abdomen, and lower back warm

overshoes keep cold and wet out

Wear a mid-layer on top of the tights, preferably one with a hood that fits under your helmet if it is very cold. Your outer layer should be long-sleeved and wind- and waterproof with tight-fitting cuffs.

Wear full-fingered winter cycling gloves on your hands. They should be made of thermal insulated material and have long cuffs that cover your wrists. Pull the sleeve of your outer or mid-layer over the glove cuff to form a seal. Finally, to protect your feet from the cold, wear thermal socks, and cover road shoes with neoprene overshoes.

Summer road clothing

Start with a thin wicking undervest. On top of this wear a lightweight short-sleeved cycling top—they have zips at the neck for extra ventilation and pockets on the back for carrying items such as food or keys. Choose one made from a fabric with good wicking qualities.

Road riders usually wear Lycra racing shorts with a padded seat, either with or without a bib over the shoulders. You can also wear baggy shorts, if preferred. Wear socks to protect your feet because there is little or no cushioning in cycling shoes. Finally, wear fingerless cycling gloves to help absorb sweat, aid grip, and protect your hands if you fall.

Layer up
In cold weather, stay warm by wearing lots of layers; several thin layers provide more insulation than two thick ones.

Stay cool
Summer clothing should be light and breathable; fabrics that don't breathe get wet with sweat and become damp and uncomfortable.

a helmet is essential; choose one with good ventilation to keep your head cool

cycling sunglasses often have replaceable lenses with different tints

this lightweight cycling top is made from a synthetic fabric but it still allows the skin to breathe

cycling gloves are cushioned to make gripping the handlebars more comfortable

cycling shorts have a padded insert which cushions your butt

road shoes have very stiff soles and no tread

Winter off-road clothing

Start with a thick base layer, preferably long-sleeved and with good wicking qualities. Then wear bib tights with a padded seat to cover the abdomen and help keep your body warm. Add a mid-layer such as a cycling-specific top with a high neck. Your outer layer should be wind and waterproof and have long sleeves with tight-fitting cuffs. If possible, wear an off-road-specific outer layer as it will be designed to cope with a wide range of conditions. Specially designed clothing is made from robust material that won't tear if it catches on thorns or branches, and it often has useful features such as pockets that can be used for maps, food, and special equipment.

Wear thermal gloves to keep your hands warm and thermal socks to insulate your feet. If necessary, cover off-road shoes with overshoes for extra protection from the cold. Consider buying special off-road winter shoes if you live in a cold climate. A thermal headband to keep the ears warm is also useful.

Summer off-road clothing

Wear a lightweight, wicking, short-sleeved base layer next to the skin. Choose a top made from similar fabric, and with rear pockets for holding food, to go over this. Then wear either Lycra road shorts or the cycling-specific baggy shorts that many mountain bikers prefer. Mountain biking shorts are made from tough, tear-resistant fabric, but because they are loose they are still quite cool in warm weather. They often have deep, zipped pockets that can be very useful.

Socks should be relatively thin, and shoes should have mesh uppers to allow your feet to breathe. Fingerless gloves help your grip and will protect your hands should you fall.

If you venture into hill country or real mountains, be aware that the weather can change very quickly. Take a lightweight, waterproof top with you, even on a warm day.

fit your helmet over a thermal hat or headband

a polo-neck will keep the cold out

gloves are full-fingered, thermal, and hard-wearing

bib tights provide padding and warmth

Protection from the elements
Off-road-specific clothing will keep you warm and dry, but it will also protect you from thorns and twigs that might otherwise scratch you.

Cool and protected
Choose loose-fitting clothing made from breathable fabrics—it allows ventilation while also protecting you from scratches on the trail.

sunglasses protect your eyes from brightness and insects

put the arms of your sunglasses over, not under, the straps of your helmet

fingerless gloves protect the hands and provide cushioning

baggy shorts allow for good ventilation

summer shoes should be well-ventilated

CYCLING INDOORS

If the weather is bad, or if it is dark outside, you might prefer to train indoors. One option is to cycle on an exercise bike or spin trainer, either at home or in the gym. The other option is to mount your outdoor bike on a turbo trainer, an apparatus that allows you to control the degree of resistance that you pedal against, and most closely simulates the feeling of riding on the road.

Choosing an exercise bike

There are many different indoor training bikes available. Even the most basic models should display distance, speed, time, calories burned, and the resistance level at which you are working. More sophisticated (and expensive) exercise bikes also offer these features, but you pay extra for more levels of resistance, pre-programed workouts, and in some cases heart-rate monitors. You don't need to spend a lot of money on a bike with lots of features. Make sure that the bike is comfortable, and that you can easily reach and read the display monitor, which will allow you to adjust the resistance as you ride. Look for a bike with a heavy front wheel as this makes it more stable, although do make sure that it has casters so that you can move it. Finally, if possible, choose an exercise bike with toe clips; these allow you to pedal more efficiently because they encourage you to pull up on the pedals as well as push down.

Correct position

Before you start your workout, make sure that the saddle height on the exercise bike is correct. This will help ensure that your leg muscles work efficiently when you pedal. See step 1 on page 30 for instructions on how to set your position.

What to wear

Wear either baggy or Lycra cycling shorts, but do ensure that they have a padded seat, even if you are just training on an exercise bike, and any top made from well-ventilated wicking material. Wear cycling-specific shoes, as these provide proper foot support. Sneakers allow your foot to curve downward when pedaling, which can cause ligament strain.

Keeping cool indoors
Indoor training can be hot and sweaty work; choose a ventilated room, use a fan or turn on the air conditioning.

EXERCISING ON A TURBO TRAINER

A turbo trainer consists of a stand on which you secure your bike, and a resistance unit. The best model is the wind trainer, where resistance is controlled by a small paddle that revolves in the air at a speed proportional to that at which you are pedaling. The harder you pedal, the faster the vanes on the paddle revolve, so wind resistance increases as you build up speed, just as it would outdoors. Useful features on a turbo trainer are speed and distance readings, and additional magnetic resistance to simulate hills.

bike support frame

resistance unit

flywheel

trainer foot

CYCLING SKILLS

If you are new to cycling, or if you have not been cycling regularly, the pages that follow will give you every basic skill that you need to take your riding to the next level. This is where you learn to set your riding position correctly to ensure comfort and to get the most from your workouts. Every cycling fundamental, from braking, changing gear and taking corners to riding on different surfaces and in traffic is covered here. I also outline the subtleties of efficient and smooth pedaling so that you use every muscle in your legs and avoid muscle cramps and tiredness when you are in the saddle.

SETTING YOUR RIDING POSITION

Once you have a bike with the right frame size for your body (*see pp.16–17*), the next step is to make the necessary adjustments to the saddle to ensure that you are correctly positioned on it. This will make the bike easier to control and enhance leg power by ensuring that your muscles work efficiently when you pedal. You'll also feel more comfortable if the height and position of your saddle are correct.

1 Support yourself against a wall, and ask someone to help by observing you. Remove one shoe and sit straight on the bike. Turn the pedal to the bottom of the revolution, and place your heel on it.

2 Raise or lower the saddle until your leg is completely straight. Your saddle is at the correct height when your leg is straight with your heel on the pedal.

3 Check that the clamp bolt under the saddle is tight, then put your shoe back on. Ask your helper to stand behind you. Ride away from your helper and ask them to check that your hips are not rocking as you pedal. If they rock at all, the saddle is too high. Go back and repeat step one.

4 Support yourself against a wall, and with your cranks parallel to the floor, place the widest part of your shoe over the pedal axle. For clip-in pedals, adjust your cleats as necessary. Then your helper checks that the end of your femur (the depression in the side of your knee) is in line with the pedal axle.

5 Brake levers should be angled so that you pull on them in line with your arms. You should also be able to apply your brakes easily with two fingers. If you are stretching too far to brake, have the reach adjusted. Follow the manufacturer's instructions or ask a bike shop if they will make the adjustment for you.

BRAKING AND CHANGING GEAR

Braking and changing gear are all about anticipation and timing. Try to be aware of what is ahead of you, and if you need to brake to reduce speed, do so while you are riding in a straight line and in plenty of time. Generally, change gears before gradients increase or decrease. Use low gears (smaller chainring, larger sprocket) for uphill, and high gears (larger chainring, smaller sprocket) for going down.

ON ROAD

Make big changes of gear ratio, as might be needed when going from flat riding to a hill, by shifting between chainrings, then fine tune by shifting between sprockets until you get a gear ratio that gives a comfortable pedal cadence. With a new bike, always establish which brake lever operates the front and rear brakes. They vary between manufacturers. However, left-hand shifters always shift between chainrings, and right between sprockets.

1 When riding on the flat, do most braking with the front brake, but use both if you have to stop quickly. The best hand position for braking on the flat, uphill, or in traffic is to hold the top of the brake hoods. Apply your brakes smoothly and with progressive force.

2 Going downhill, it is best to apply the brakes with your hands in a lower position. This gives you more leverage when you brake. On gentle gradients, use your front brake, but on steeper ones use your back brake, too. Emphasize the back brake more on steeper gradients.

Shimano shifters
Move the brake lever in to go up a gear; use a second lever to go down.

3 On Campagnolo brake/shift systems, push the lever behind the brake lever to shift from smaller to larger chainrings/sprockets; shift to smaller chainrings/sprockets by pressing a lever on the inner side of the brake hood. On Shimano systems (inset), shift to larger chainrings/sprockets by pushing the whole brake lever inward; shift to smaller chainrings/sprockets by pressing a lever behind the brake lever inward.

4 With the Campagnolo system, it is possible to shift across several sprockets at once with one move of the shift lever. However, with the Shimano system, this is only possible when going from smaller to larger sprockets—when shifting in the opposite direction, you must click the lever several times.

5 Keep pedaling whenever you shift gear, and with integrated brake/shift systems, as shown here, you can shift gear while riding out of the saddle. Ease your pedaling a fraction when making such a shift. Only stop pedaling to shift gear with hub gears, which are quite rare.

OFF ROAD

Loose and uneven surfaces on off-road terrain mean that you need to brake earlier than when riding on road, and be even smoother when applying your brakes. Suddenly grabbing at your brakes will almost certainly cause your wheels to lock on loose surfaces. Stay in the saddle when pedaling uphill on loose surfaces, as this will increase your rear wheel traction; use a lower gear than you would to tackle the hill out of the saddle.

1 When riding on flat terrain, do most of your braking with your front brake, as it is more powerful than the rear one and more sensitive. Use the rear brake as well as the front if you need more stopping power. Apply brakes with two fingers, leaving two to hold the handlebars.

2 Use the rear brake more when descending. Use it in conjunction with the front, but switch emphasis to the rear if the down gradient increases. Relying too much on the front brake on a steep descent shifts weight over the front wheel, and the rear one can lift off the ground.

pull this lever to shift to a smaller chainring or sprocket

3 Most off-road bikes have Rapid-fire shifters. Push the lower lever with your thumb to shift to a larger chainring or sprocket. To shift to a smaller chainring or sprocket, pull the upper lever inward with your index finger.

4 Different shaped teeth on chainrings and sprockets facilitate smooth gear shifts. As you shift from smaller to larger chainrings, reduce the amount of pressure you apply to the pedals, but don't stop pedaling.

5 For the most efficient gear ratios, avoid combining the largest chainring with the largest sprockets, and smallest chainring with the smallest sprockets. Bike chains are flexible, but they work best when they are in as near to a straight line as possible.

6 You can shift gears while riding out of the saddle, but ease off a fraction on the pedals during the shift, especially on bumpy off-road terrain. This applies when shifting up as well as down. Never shift chainrings and sprockets at the same time.

CORNERING

Safe and efficient cornering depends on the line that you take through a corner and on subtle changes in the way that you position your body on the bike. Your approach line into a corner determines where you will come out on the road. Changes in body position redistribute your weight to help lead you through the corner while maintaining balance and control.

TAKING AN ON-ROAD CORNER

Take corners slowly in traffic. When there is no traffic you can corner with more speed, but do take care to come out of the corner on the correct side of the road. When making a turn that involves crossing a road to a corner on the opposite side to you, start from the inner edge of your side and corner in a wide arc so that you avoid any oncoming traffic from the road into which you are turning. Always indicate before a turn (*see pp.44–45*).

1 To turn a corner on your side of the road, first look over your opposite shoulder to check on traffic conditions. When turning your head, there may be a tendency to steer in the direction that you look. Relax the arm on that side to prevent this from happening.

2 If the traffic is clear, move out toward the center of the road to allow you to take a straighter line through the corner. Then brake to slow down to the speed at which you will take the corner. Shift to a lower gear now if the road ascends after the corner.

3 Stop pedaling and lean the bike into the corner. Keep your inside foot at the top of the pedal revolution to prevent the pedal from catching the road. Point your inside knee into the corner and move your weight over your outside leg. Aim your bike to brush the inside of the corner just after its apex.

4 Once out of the corner, and when you are riding straight with your bike upright, stand up on the pedals and accelerate away. Be sure to correct your position on the road before you accelerate.

TAKING AN OFF-ROAD CORNER

Off-road, the quickest way to get around a corner is to start wide, cut across the middle, and come out of it wide. With no traffic off-road, you can have fun with this technique—use more of the road to turn, and maintain at least moderate speed. Be aware of trail conditions though—don't pick a line that crosses a loose surface just because it is quickest. Be sure to ride conservatively and be considerate to other trail users.

1 Check behind and in front of you before you move into position to turn the corner, and assess the best line of attack. For a right turn, move toward the left of the trail, then brake to reduce your speed. Make any gear changes necessary for after the corner.

2 Stop pedaling with your inside pedal up to prevent it from catching on the ground. Lean into the corner, and turn, pointing your inside knee out slightly, into the corner, to transfer some of your weight into it and help guide the bike around the corner.

3 Cut the corner at its apex. Shift your body weight over your outside leg to control your bike and prevent it from drifting out. If you are turning too tightly, pull your inside knee in slightly. If you are going too wide, shift more weight over your outside leg. Keep your arms relaxed to absorb bumps from uneven terrain.

4 Once you are around the corner and your bike is moving straight, get out of the saddle and push on the pedals to accelerate. Make sure that your bike is vertical before you start pedaling.

EFFICIENT PEDALING

To pedal efficiently, you must make subtle adjustments to the angle of your foot to ensure that power is transferred to the pedals throughout the entire revolution. This increases the number of leg muscles that you use in each rotation and will maximize the benefits you get from cycling. Don't worry if it looks complicated—it feels a very natural process and comes easily with practice.

1 Push the pedal slightly forward before you push down—it is difficult to push downward with the pedal at the top of the revolution. In this phase you use your thigh muscles.

slight forward motion

2 As the pedal moves forward from the top of the revolution, drop your heel slightly to help your leg push forward and down. Your thigh and shin muscles work together to power this phase of the revolution.

push

3 As the revolution continues, the muscles in your buttocks, hip, and thigh push the pedal down, helped by your calves as your toes drop below your heel. This is the most powerful phase of the pedal revolution.

push

4 At the bottom of the stroke you cannot push down further, so pull back on the pedal. This action is like scraping something off the bottom of your shoe, and you use your hamstrings and calf muscles to perform it.

5 Relax the muscles of your recovering leg when riding fast on the flat during this phase. When pedaling slowly, or when riding uphill or out of the saddle, there is more of a pull to this phase, and you use your hip, hamstrings, and calf muscles.

6 Toward the end of the revolution, begin to push the pedal forward. With practice you will be able to time this forward push effort so that it does not create tension in the muscles of the recovering leg.

SAFETY

Awareness is your key to safety. Be aware of changing road and trail conditions and of other users and their rights and needs. Never second guess another person's movements. If you haven't cycled for a while, consider taking some lessons. Otherwise, if you are not familiar with your bike, practice riding it on a stretch of little-used, flat terrain before you head out onto the open road or trails.

RIDING AT NIGHT

I do not recommend that you train in the dark. If you have to cycle at night, it is essential that you take every measure to make yourself as visible as possible.

In many countries you must have rear and front lights by law, but to be really safe, consider adding constant LED (light-emitting diode) lights to traditional bike lights and clipping flashing LEDs to your clothing. Wear clothing with reflective strips, particularly on your legs, and reflectors that fit onto your spokes, as these help identify you as a cyclist to other road users.

Training in the dark on an unlit road is, obviously, dangerous. If you live in the countryside, train indoors when you cannot ride in daylight. In towns and cities, business parks offer wide, well-lit and less trafficked roads, especially after working hours, which can be suitable for training.

HAZARDOUS ROAD SURFACES

There are techniques for dealing with different road surfaces and riding conditions. Dismount rather than take an unnecessary risk.

Painted road markings become slippery in wet conditions. Avoid riding over them, if possible; otherwise, ride over them slowly or approach at as near to a 90° angle as you can, preferably both.

Cobblestones are still a feature of many European cities. Before a short stretch of cobbles, raise yourself out of the saddle, stop pedaling, keep your weight back and let the flex on your arms and legs absorb the bumps. For longer stretches, sit well back in the saddle and keep pedaling hard. In the rain, cobblestones can become particularly treacherous and slippery. Be sure to take corners especially slowly when riding on wet cobbles.

Tramlines are best avoided. You will crash if one of your wheels drops into a tramline. If you absolutely have to cross them, approach with a little speed and at a 90° angle.

Wet conditions make nearly all surfaces that you ride on slippery. This is particularly true of roads, especially after a spell of dry weather. Oil spillages from traffic build up when it is dry, and the first rain can make road surfaces ice-like. Watch for the tell-tale rainbow effect of oil on water, and avoid riding through it. Avoid puddles, since they can hide potholes. Never ride on icy roads.

SAFETY IN TRAFFIC

Before venturing into traffic, make sure that you can maneuvre your bike at slow speeds without wobbling, and can look left and right behind you while traveling in a straight line. Practice these skills on quiet roads. Ride with courtesy, and respect other road users but don't be tentative. Never take for granted what other road users will do. Remember the following key safety points when riding in traffic.

SET OFF SAFELY

Before you set off, look over your shoulder to check on traffic conditions behind you. Once there is a gap in the traffic big enough for you to fit in, indicate with a hand signal that you intend to set off, then move into the traffic. Use a low gear when setting off as there can be a tendency to wobble when using a high one.

BE AWARE IN TRAFFIC

When you are riding along in traffic, keep checking on what is happening around you. Look for indicator lights on vehicles, and watch drivers waiting in side streets to pull out—be wary and get ready to brake if they are not looking at you. Ride at a steady pace, not too slowly and certainly not too fast, although a little speed can help to keep you balanced.

KEEP CONTROL

Keep two or three fingers on your brake levers on a hybrid or mountain bike, so that you are ready to brake. On a road bike, ride with your hands on top of the brake hoods to ensure that you don't have to reach far to brake. Shift to a low gear if you have to slow down or stop—that way you will be ready to set off again.

KEEP DISTANCE

Give the vehicle in front space to stop when you are both traveling at the same speed, but do not drop too far back or you will be overtaken. Similarly, don't race to keep up, let traffic flow past.

SIGNAL

Signal every time you maneuvre. Look behind, decide what speed you need to make the maneuvre safely, then brake well before you signal. If it is safe to go, make your signal but be confident and obvious—extend your arm and point with your finger. Check behind again, and if it is safe to do so, make your manuevre.

CHECK BEHIND

Before you make any change in direction, check behind you. Do this often in any case. Be aware that there is a tendency to steer towards the side you are checking—relax the arm on that side to prevent this.

FITNESS, DIET, AND EXERCISE

Research into improving how athletes train has given us

a better understanding of how to exercise in a structured

way that is guaranteed to bring improvements. We also know

that in order to see results, any training program must be

combined with a balanced diet. In these pages I outline the

training and diet principles that underpin the Program.

I cover the basics of warming up and offer essential stretches

for cooling down after a cycling session. I have also included

key exercises for the abdomen, lower back, and upper body.

Complete the fitness test at the end of this section to establish

the level at which you should undertake the Program.

PRINCIPLES OF TRAINING

To benefit most from the Program, you need to be aware of your heart rate while exercising. This helps you to understand how your body is responding to different degrees of exertion and ensures that you can exercise at the level that most efficiently works your heart and lungs. Familiarize yourself with the different training levels, and understand how your body performs as you push it to work harder.

Building fitness

The training program featured in this book focuses on two main components of fitness. The first is aerobic, or cardiovascular, exercise, which improves the efficiency and capacity of your circulatory system: Your heart, lungs, and blood vessels. Very simply, this is exercise that raises your heart rate. The second component is muscle fitness. The actions of pedaling and gripping the handlebars strengthen, tone, and shape your muscles because they must work against resistance.

Working with training levels

During the Program, you train at different intensities to build aerobic fitness. (*See* Using Training Levels, *right*.) These intensities are determined by percentages of your maximum heart rate (MHR). Work out your MHR by subtracting your age from 220. By this calculation, a 36-year-old has a MHR of 184 beats per minute (BPM). To work out your target heart rate for each of the five training zones, multiply your MHR by 0.6, 0.7, 0.75, 0.8 and 0.85.

When you are cycling, you can be sure that you are working at the correct heart rate by using a heart-rate monitor (*see opposite*), or by taking your pulse manually (although this will mean that you have to stop, so you won't get a very accurate reading). You can also use the talking index (*see right*) as a fairly accurate and convenient method for gauging the level at which you are working.

USING TRAINING LEVELS

Intensity	Target heart rate (% MHR)	Talking index
Active recovery	60–70	Able to converse as normal
Stamina booster	70–75	Short breath needed after every sentence
Utilization	75–80	Deep breath needed after every sentence
Threshold	80–85	Deep breath needed after three or four words
Capacity	85 and over	Unable to speak

Active recovery is the level of exercise that you do the day after a hard session. This gentle exercise helps your body to recover and rebuild.

Stamina booster is the level of exercise that builds basic aerobic fitness. It strengthens the heart and stimulates the growth of blood capillaries; as a result, more oxygen can be circulated to the muscles throughout the body.

Utilization is the level of exercise at which the muscles become more efficient at taking up and processing the oxygen they receive via the heart and circulatory system.

Threshold is the hardest level at which you can exercise constantly. The body can still reprocess the lactic acid that is produced as a by-product of strenuous exercise.

Capacity is the hardest level at which you can exercise using oxygen, or aerobically. Above this level you work anaerobically and not enough oxygen reaches the muscles.

CYCLE COMPUTER

This is a useful and inexpensive device that will allow you to time your rides by recording your speed and distance. More sophisticated models can display your current, average, and maximum speeds. Regularly riding a decided route and comparing your times is a good way to measure improvements in your fitness.

Using a heart-rate monitor
A strap worn around the chest monitors your heart and sends a signal to a small device that can be worn on the wrist (as shown here) or mounted on the handlebars of the bike. It displays a continuous reading of your heart rate.

Taking your pulse manually
Place your first two fingers on the artery just below your jaw bone. Count your pulse for 15 seconds, then multiply by 4 to give the number of BPM.

DIET AND NUTRITION

To get the most from the Program, or any exercise regime, it is important to support your training by eating a healthy and balanced diet. Be aware of the different food groups, learn how they nourish and fuel the body, and aim to incorporate them into your diet every day. Note that you should adjust the quantity that you eat in accordance with your exercise levels and eat less on non-training days.

Carbohydrates

The body breaks carbohydrates down into glucose, which it uses as a source of energy for our muscles. There are two types of carbohydrate: Simple and complex. Because of their more complicated structure, complex carbohydrates take longer to break down so energy is released at a slow but steady rate. Good sources of complex carbohydrates include whole wheat bread and pasta, beans, basmati rice, couscous, and bulgar wheat. These are ideal foods to eat to help the body meet the long-term energy demands of cycling. Simple carbohydrates, which are basically sugar, are broken down quickly and supply the body with a quick rush of energy, but this will be followed by an energy low. Try

Eat well, perform better
Snack on fresh fruit, include oily fish in your diet, since it contains nutrients and "good fats," and choose whole wheat bread over white.

to avoid eating sweet snacks such as cookies and chocolate bars. Avoid sugary carbonated drinks, too.

Proteins

Our digestive systems break proteins down into amino acids, which our bodies use as building blocks to repair tissue and build new muscles. Animal protein contains all the amino acids the body needs, but vegetarians must combine different foods to ensure they get all the essential amino acids. Good combinations are corn with beans, or rice with peas, or lentils with bread. Meat, cheese, beans, eggs, seeds, and nuts are all good sources of protein.

Fats

There are "good" fats (unsaturated) and "bad" fats (saturated). Unsaturated fats are an essential part

of our diets; they can be used as fuel, especially for long duration, low-level activities. They help the body absorb essential vitamins from other food sources. Saturated fats, on the other hand, slow the metabolism, raise blood cholesterol levels, and are linked to high blood pressure and heart disease. As a general guide, bad fats are usually solid at room temperature, and good fats are liquid. So the fat around meat is bad for you, and should be avoided, but olive oil is good. Watch out for hidden bad fats in foods such as cakes, biscuits, and processed foods. Read labels, and avoid foods that contain significant amounts of saturated fat.

Vitamins and minerals

These nutrients are found in a variety of foods, and are essential for growth, rejuvenation, and certain metabolic processes. They are often destroyed by cooking and storage, so include plenty of fresh food in your diet. Raw fruit and vegetables are excellent sources of vitamins and minerals.

Nourishment to support training

Whether you are following the Program or training for a big race, be sure to eat a healthy diet to help fuel your body for optimum performance. Keep the following diet advice in mind when training:
• Include foods from each group in your daily diet, in a ratio in weight of roughly five parts carbohydrate, to two of protein, to one of fat. (But remember, eat only good fats, and try to eliminate bad ones altogether.)
• Aim to eat at least five portions of fresh fruit and vegetables per day. A portion is one piece of fruit or about three heaped tablespoons of vegetables. You can include fruit juice as one portion of fruit, regardless of the quantity that you drink.
• Try to have five smaller meals a day rather than three big ones, and keep intake of simple carbohydrates to a minimum. This will prevent

---

DIET AND TRAINING GOALS

Generally speaking, if you follow the Program and support your training by eating a healthy, balanced diet as outlined on these pages, you will lose weight. Most nutritionists agree that the best way to lose weight is to reduce the quantities that you eat and increase the amount of exercise that you do. Here I outline ways in which you can make subtle changes to your diet to help you to meet different training goals.

To help weight loss: At all meals, reduce the amount of carbohydrate that you eat and increase your intake of fresh fruit and vegetables. The ideal portions on your plate should be half vegetables, one quarter carbohydrate, and one quarter protein.

When your weight has reduced, slowly increase the quantity of carbohydrate that you eat until it is in balance with the amount of energy that you expend. This occurs when you reach a balance point where you neither gain nor lose weight. Weigh yourself regularly, but only adjust your diet in response to trends, not individual readings.

To build muscle: Eat a balanced, healthy diet as outlined here, but increase your intake of protein so that you eat 0.07oz (2g) for every 2.2lb (1kg) of your body weight every day.

To complete a long-distance ride: Eat plenty of complex carbohydrates such as pasta, bread, and rice on the day before your ride to give your energy reserves a boost.

---

energy highs and lows that can reduce your ability to train properly.
• To help you recover after training, try to have a snack of protein and carbohydrate in the thirty minutes following a session. Your body's ability to process carbohydrates increases just after exercise, and combining carbohydrates with protein increases the speed of their absorption still further.
• Finally, but most importantly, keep hydrated. Drink water, or a sports drink, during exercise, and sip water all day. Try to drink at least 2 liters (4 pints) a day, more if it is hot.

WARMING UP, COOLING DOWN

Ease your body into any cycling session by taking at least ten minutes to warm up. In the Program, you always begin by cycling slowly and then gradually increase the intensity. To aid recovery after a session, always cool down by riding the last five to ten minutes of it in a low gear, gradually reducing your effort. Then perform the sequence of simple stretches demonstrated here.

CALF STRETCH

This stretch improves range of movement in the calf and ankle and will help you to pedal more efficiently. It also helps squeeze waste products from the calf.

HAMSTRING STRETCH

The one muscle that doesn't get fully stretched during cycling is the hamstring in the backs of the legs. Perform this simple stretch to prevent tightness and imbalances.

QUAD STRETCH

The quadriceps, the muscles at the fronts of the thighs, work hard when you cycle. This stretch helps reduce tightness and also squeezes waste products from them.

Stand with your feet together, then step back with your right foot and bend your left leg slightly. Keep your back straight, and push back into your right heel, keeping it on the ground, until you feel a good stretch in your right calf. Hold for a count of 10, then stretch your left calf.

Stand with your feet together, then place your right heel in front of you and straighten your right leg. Bend your left, supporting leg slightly and bend forward from your hips until you feel a stretch in the back of your right leg. Hold for a count of 10, then stretch your left hamstring.

Stand up straight, hold the front of your right foot, and pull your right heel to your buttock. Keep your knees together and your left, supporting leg slightly bent. Feel a stretch in the front of your right thigh. Hold for a count of 10, then stretch your left quadricep.

UPPER BACK STRETCH

The muscles in your upper back that pull your shoulder blades together work hard when you cycle, especially when riding off-road. This will help ease tension.

CHEST STRETCH

The muscles in your chest and shoulders can become tense from holding the handlebars in front of your body. This stretches them out and reduces tension.

Stand with your feet hip-width apart and your knees slightly bent. Clasp your hands in front of you at chest level. Gently pull your shoulders back as you push your hands away from you. Keep your lower back firm and your body upright. Feel a stretch across your back and into your shoulders. Hold for a count of 10.

Stand with your feet hip-width apart and your knees slightly bent. Clasp your hands behind your back and, keeping your back straight and your abdominals firm, lift your arms until you feel a stretch across your chest. Pull your shoulders back slightly to intensify the stretch. Hold for a count of 10.

CORE EXERCISES

The aim of these exercises is to build core strength, a term that refers to the muscles of your abdominals and back and their ability to support your spine. Cycling improves core strength—keeping your balance on a bike and pedaling engage your core muscles—but these exercises will support that work. Aim to perform these exercises as part of every cycling session.

OBLIQUE CRUNCH

This exercise helps to strengthen and tone the obliques, the muscles that run along the sides of the stomach. Remember to breathe out as you execute the crunch and to breathe in as you come back down.

1 Lie on a mat with your knees bent and feet flat on the floor. Place your hands by your head with your elbows pointing to the sides.

2 Slowly raise your left elbow and shoulder off the mat, and lift them toward your right knee. Then slowly lower them back down to the mat. Feel this in your left oblique. Lift your right elbow and shoulder up toward your left knee to work your right oblique.

LOWER BACK STRENGTHENER

Back pain often occurs when the larger surface muscles in the back become dominant and put pressure on the spine, pulling it out of line. This exercise stimulates and strengthens the small muscles close to the spine, keeping them healthy and increasing their ability to support the spine and hold it in line.

1 Lie on your back with your knees bent and your feet flat on the floor about hip-width apart. Relax your arms at your sides and turn your hands so that your palms face down. Press your lower back into the floor.

2 Slowly raise your hips by curling your spine upward. Starting with the lowest, lift your vertebra off the floor one at a time. Concentrate on keeping the movement slow and controlled.

3 Continue raising your hips until they are in line with your knees—don't raise them higher than this. Then slowly lower your hips vertebra by vertebra, this time starting at the top of your spine, until you return to the start position.

UPPER BODY EXERCISES

Although your legs do most of the work when you cycle, if you're new to it you'll be surprised by how tired your arms and shoulders get, especially when riding off-road or out of the saddle. Most of the sessions in the Program strengthen and tone all the muscles of your body, but sometimes I'll suggest that you perform one of these simple upper body exercises to complete the workout.

LATERAL RAISE

Feel this exercise in your shoulder muscles. Take care to keep your back straight and your head up as you lift the weights. Inhale as you make the effort to lift the weights and exhale as you lower them.

1 Stand with your feet hip-width apart and your knees slightly bent. Hold the weights at your sides with your palms facing inward. Keep your abdominals firm.

2 Slowly raise the weights to shoulder level at your sides, keeping your arms straight. Your palms should face downward; don't allow your hands to twist. Then slowly lower the weights to your sides again.

BICEPS CURL

Keep your back straight and your torso firm as you perform this exercise. Inhale as you lift the weight, exhale as you lower it.

1 Stand with your feet hip-width apart and your knees slightly bent. Hold the weights at your sides so that your palms face outward.

2 Slowly lift the right weight toward your right shoulder. Take care to keep your right elbow tucked into your body and your back straight. Then slowly lower the weight back down again. Repeat with your left arm.

SHOULDER PRESS

Feel this exercise in your shoulders and in the backs of your upper arms. Focus on keeping the movement slow and controlled.

1 Sit on a bench. Hold a weight in each hand and bend your arms at 90° so that your elbows are at shoulder level.

2 Slowly raise the weights straight up above your shoulders. Take care to keep your back straight and your body still. Don't lock your arms straight, but keep them slightly bent. Then slowly lower the weights back down to the start position.

HOW FIT ARE YOU?

The fitness test below establishes your current level of fitness by evaluating your aerobic health, physical strength, and body proportions. Calculate your results by referring to the box opposite, and find the level at which you should follow the Program: Beginner, Intermediate, or Advanced. Make a note of your results so that you can compare them when you come back to take the test again.

THE FITNESS TEST

Body Mass Index (BMI)

This test helps determine how healthy your body shape is by assessing your weight in relation to your height.

Calculate your BMI by dividing your weight in kilograms by your height in metres squared (1lb = 0.45kg, 1ft = 30.48cm, 1in = 2.5cm).

For example, if you weigh 53kg and are 1.62m tall, calculate your height squared (1.62 × 1.62), then divide 53 by 2.62 to give you a BMI of 20.2.

a **Female**: 26.1 or more; **Male**: 26.1 or more
b **Female**: 21–26; **Male**: 21–26
c **Female**: up to 20.9; **Male**: up to 20.9

Hip-to-waist ratio

This test assesses how healthy your body shape is with regard to fat distribution. Most people store body fat around the waist and hips.

Calculate your hip-to-waist ratio by measuring your hips (just below the top of your pelvis) and then your waist (around your middle, going over your belly button). Divide your waist measurement by your hip measurement (using either metric or imperial measurements).

a **Female**: above 0.86; **Male**: above 0.95
b **Female**: 0.71–0.85; **Male**: 0.81–0.94
c **Female**: below 0.7; **Male**: below 0.8

One-minute push-up test

This tests upper body strength. Do as many push-ups (either the full or easier half variety, see *opposite*) as you can in one minute. Note, that when you repeat this test, you should perform the same type of push-up. If you can't do a full minute of push-ups, count the number that you successfully complete.

Full push-ups (results for half push-ups in brackets)
a **Female**: 4 or less (24 or less); **Male**: 9 or less (29 or less)
b **Female**: 5–15 (25–40); **Male**: 10–30 (30–50)
c **Female**: 16 or more (41 or more); **Male**: 31 or more (51 or more)

One-minute crunch test

This tests abdominal, or stomach muscle, strength. Do as many crunches (see *opposite*) as you can in one minute.

a **Female**: 24 or less; **Male**: 24 or less
b **Female**: 25–45; **Male**: 25–45
c **Female**: 46 or more; **Male**: 46 or more

Three-minute step test

This tests aerobic, or cardiovascular, fitness. Do step-ups (see *opposite*) at a rate of 30 steps per minute for three minutes. Stop and take your pulse for 15 seconds, then multiply the figure by 4 to give your number of heart beats per minute.

a **Female**: 167 or more; **Male**: 157 or more
b **Female**: 141–166; **Male**: 131–156
c **Female**: 128–140; **Male**: 120–130

PUSH-UP

If you can't do a full push-up, do the easier half version with knees on the ground. Keep your bottom tucked in. Remember to inhale as you lower yourself down, and exhale as you make the effort to press up.

1 Place your hands under your shoulders with fingers pointing forward. Keep your torso and legs straight. If performing a half push-up, start with your knees on the floor and your feet raised.

2 Slowly lower your body to the floor until your arms are bent at 90°. Take care to keep your legs and torso straight and not to push your butt into the air. Then push yourself back up to start position.

CRUNCH

A common mistake with the crunch is to yank your head up with your hands. Remember, this exercise targets the abdominals, so you should feel it there. Exhale as you curl up, and inhale as you lower yourself down.

1 Lie on your back with your knees bent and your feet flat on the floor. Place your hands by your head so that your elbows point out to the sides. Keep your lower back in contact with the mat.

2 Tense your abdominals and curl your shoulders forward so that they come off the mat. Don't pull your head forward with your hands. Then slowly lower your shoulders back down to the start position.

STEP-UP

Use a step or bench that you can step up onto comfortably—your knee shouldn't bend to less than 90°.

Stand facing the bench. Step up with one foot, then with the other, so that both feet are on the bench. Step down with one foot, then the other. Keep your back straight.

FITNESS TEST RESULTS

a = 1 pt **b** = 2 pts **c** = 3 pts

5 to 8
Beginner level. You need to make a concerted effort to improve your fitness. You could benefit immensely from the Program.

9 to 13
Intermediate level. You have a good base level of fitness, but by following the Program you could look and feel even better.

14 to 18
Advanced level. You are in good shape, but the Program should still challenge you; enjoy meeting new fitness goals.

THE PROGRAM

In the pages that follow I present my seven-week program for getting fit through cycling. This training program has been devised to build fitness by strengthening your heart and lungs while also toning and shaping the muscles of your lower and upper body. Each week's structured sessions provide good workouts, but they were also designed to be fun and varied. As your fitness level improves, you practice and hone your riding skills which will help you to explore new terrains as well as increase the effectiveness and quality of each workout. Before starting, be sure to complete the Fitness Test (see *pp.58–59*) to establish the level at which you should follow the Program.

FOLLOWING THE PROGRAM

You are about to use cycling to become fitter, more toned, and stronger. Follow this Program and see how regular cycling workouts can increase your aerobic fitness, build strength, and focus you mentally. Follow the Program from start to finish and you will discover how riding your bike can be an enjoyable pastime as well as a rewarding workout.

How the program works

The seven-week Program consists of two three-week blocks where you train for four sessions a week. The blocks are separated by a week where you train for three sessions but also do the Bike Test (*see opposite*) to evaluate your progress. In the first three-week block, the focus is on building stamina, so you work at a low percentage of your maximum heart rate (MHR) (*see pp.48–49*). As the Program progresses, you work at a higher percentage of MHR to increase your fitness while still developing stamina.

All sessions consist of a warm-up, where you gradually raise your heart rate; the main work part, where you train at the specific intensities that achieve the objective of the session; and a cool-down, where you gradually lower your heart rate to help you recover. Following some sessions I recommend doing an additional upper body exercise. For these, choose a weight where you can just comfortably complete all of the repetitions (reps) with good form. Never compromise form in order to complete the reps. At the end of each session, complete the core exercises, then finish by stretching.

Before you begin the Program, determine the level at which you should follow it by completing the Fitness Test on pages 58–59. Then, before you start session one, do the Bike Test (*see opposite*).

Suitable for any bike

All the sessions can be followed on any bike—road, mountain, hybrid, or even exercise bike. On an indoor bike, adjust the pedaling resistance to achieve the specified heart rate/exercise intensity. Some advanced exercise bikes simulate changes in terrain. Where necessary, I have included special instructions for adapting the session for indoor bike use.

Session information

For each session, a box provides essential information about that day's training.

Take off on the road to fitness
Cycle with a friend or enjoy training on your own.

Length: This is the minimum duration of the cycling part of the session, including the warm-up and cool-down. It does not include the ten or so minutes that it takes to complete the core exercises, any upper body exercise, and the cool-down stretches.

Terrain: This tells you the ideal terrain for following the session. For example, hilly, flat, or undulating.

Type: For each session, you work within different heart-rate zones, and this refers to the type of training technique that you use: Constant pace, interval, or sprint training (*see below*). Use the graphs as a visual reminder of the heart-rate pattern you are aiming to achieve in each session.

Intensity: The Program provides a full-body workout. Each session has an aerobic benefit and also targets muscles in the upper and lower body. The intensities of each of these elements vary and are rated next to the relevant icons (*see box, right*).

What to do if you miss a session

In an ideal world you would never miss a session, but sometimes it will be hard not to. If you miss one session, it isn't a problem, just continue with the week. If you miss two sessions, repeat that week before moving on to the next.

THE BIKE TEST

Use this test to establish your starting point before you embark on the Program. Repeat the test after week three and again when you finish the Program to measure improvement. Choose a circuit or stretch of road or trail that is 3 miles (4.8km) long, and record the time it takes you to ride the distance at your limit. If you do not reach 80–85% MHR, you are not trying hard enough.

- Warm up with 20 minutes' progressively harder riding until you reach high intensity.

- Start your stopwatch and heart-rate monitor and ride the course or stretch of road at your limit.

- Record your time and warm down with 20 minutes of low-intensity riding in a low gear.

SESSION INFORMATION ICONS

Icons in each session's information box show how challenging the elements of the session will be. One circle indicates the lowest intensity, three circles indicate the highest.

♥ **Aerobic**: Works the heart and lungs

Lower body: Targets the legs and butt

Upper body: Works the chest, shoulders, and arms

TRAINING TECHNIQUES

For each session you work within different heart-rate zones to vary the training effect. If you're a beginner, you might find it difficult to control your heart rate to this degree to start with. This will become easier as your level of fitness improves. The graphs below illustrate the effects that the different training techniques have on your heart rate.

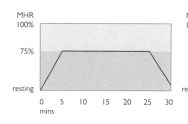

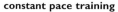

constant pace training

A short warm-up to 75% MHR, then maintaining it for 20 mins. Finally, a cool-down.

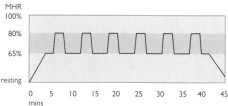

interval training

A short warm-up to 65% MHR, maintaining it briefly, building to 80% MHR and holding that briefly. 5 repeats like this, then a cool-down.

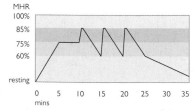

sprint training

A short warm-up to 75% MHR, holding it, then 3 short sprints and recovery. Finally, a cool-down.

WEEK ONE OVERVIEW

Your aim in this first week of the Program is to build basic aerobic fitness. The focus is on working at 70–75% MHR, or stamina-booster level (*see pp.48–49*), in order to develop this. You will repeat work at this fairly low percentage of MHR as part of almost every session. This week you also target your fast-twitch muscle fibers to help shape and tone your muscles.

Starting out

There are four sessions to complete in Week One. In these early stages of the Program, always take a day to rest between each training session to give your body a chance to recover. I planned the Program so that you do your first session on Monday, complete two further ones during the week, and then finish by riding your longest session on a Sunday. However it is not essential that you complete the sessions in this order. You can swap them around to fit your life and your schedule. Having said that, this week Session One should always be completed first.

Working at 70–75% MHR (stamina-booster level) is the key to building aerobic fitness. It is only when you can maintain this level of exercise for extended periods that you can begin to work at higher intensities and develop your fitness level further.

If you are embarking on this program after a period of inactivity, or have a low level of fitness, you may well feel tired at the end of this week, but I hope that you will also feel invigorated and focused. If you find this week very hard, try doing a 20–30-minute ride at an easy pace and taking one or two days of rest before doing another easy ride. When you can cope with cycling for 30 minutes every other day, start the Program.

Embarking on the program
Each training session takes you one step closer to improved health and fitness; this is the start of the journey.

WEEK ONE AT A GLANCE

Mon   Session 1: Stamina Booster
- Constant pace.
- A straightforward ride intended to get you used to working at stamina-booster level, or 70–75% MHR.
- The key today is to stay in control.

Tues ■ Complete rest.

Weds Session 2: Quick Spin
- Sprint training.
- Some stamina-booster work, but with at least two sprint efforts so you specifically target your fast-twitch muscles for the first time in the Program.

Thurs ■ Complete rest.

Fri   Session 3: Power Pushes
- Sprint training.
- More stamina-booster work, but hard pedaling and bike control add a muscle-toning and strengthening element to this session.

Sat   ■ Complete rest.

Sun   Session 4: Long Leisurely Ride
- Constant pace.
- Your longest ride so far. This session focuses on stamina-booster work, but you incorporate different terrains into the ride to provide an element of resistance training.

WEEK ONE: SESSION ONE

STAMINA BOOSTER

The aim of your first session is to experience the feeling of riding at the stamina-booster level, or 70–75% MHR. This intensity of work underpins the entire Program; it builds endurance and helps to develop aerobic fitness.

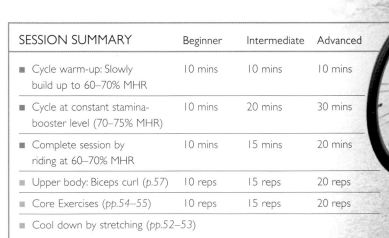

SESSION INFORMATION		
length	beg	30 mins
	int	45 mins
	adv	1hr
type	constant pace	
terrain	flat or undulating	
intensity	♥ ●●○	⚙ ●●○ 🏃 ●○○

Begin by riding at 60–70% MHR, slowly increasing your pace over 10 minutes. Then ride at 70–75% MHR for the time specified in the session summary for your fitness level. Ride on a flat or undulating course, and learn to use your gears to control the difficulty of the session, especially when cycling up hill (*see opposite*). Ensure that your heart rate does not exceed 75% MHR. Select a gear that will allow you to stay seated, since riding out of the saddle is strenuous and will increase your heart rate. Don't push yourself too hard—going above 75% MHR will reduce the beneficial effects of this session. The aim is to develop basic endurance at this level before moving on to work at higher intensities. Complete the remainder of the session by cycling at 60–70% MHR for the time specified in the summary.

> **TIP**
> Breathe deeply, and stay relaxed. Visualize the oxygen that you take in through your lungs being pumped around your body by your heart. Efficient delivery of oxygen to working muscles is what this session is all about.

SESSION SUMMARY	Beginner	Intermediate	Advanced
■ Cycle warm-up: Slowly build up to 60–70% MHR	10 mins	10 mins	10 mins
■ Cycle at constant stamina-booster level (70–75% MHR)	10 mins	20 mins	30 mins
■ Complete session by riding at 60–70% MHR	10 mins	15 mins	20 mins
■ Upper body: Biceps curl (*p.57*)	10 reps	15 reps	20 reps
■ Core Exercises (*pp.54–55*)	10 reps	15 reps	20 reps
■ Cool down by stretching (*pp.52–53*)			

Enjoying a relaxed ride
Cycling at stamina-booster level builds basic fitness and prepares your body for work at higher intensities.

TECHNIQUE: SHIFTING GEAR UPHILL

To help pace yourself, learn to make gear shifts that reflect the terrain on which you are riding. Efficient gear changes will also help to control your heart rate—using too high a gear will raise it, while one that is too low will let it drop. Try to shift gears in anticipation of terrain changes, not when you are riding over them. Use a high gear for going uphill, a lower one for going down.

1 Ride relaxed. If you are on a road bike, cycle with your hands on top of the handlebars. Make sure that you feel comfortable. If you are tense, it will push up your heart rate and reduce your pedaling efficiency.

gear shift
change gears on a hybrid bike by pressing this lever forward

keep shoulders relaxed

2 Shift gear before any changes in gradient. Use a low gear (smaller chainring, larger sprockets) for uphill and a higher one for down. Be sure to keep pedaling when you shift gear.

3 You may need to shift gear again if the gradient changes on a hill or descent. On steep climbs, sit further back in the saddle and pull hard on the handlebars to help put more power into your pedaling.

other useful techniques braking and changing gear *pp.32–35* efficient pedaling *pp.40–41*

WEEK ONE: SESSION TWO

QUICK SPIN

This session consists of a series of efforts where you pedal very quickly in a low gear, which is known as "spinning." This targets the fast-twitch muscle fibers in your legs, helping to tone and shape them. Good pedaling technique is essential (*see opposite*).

SESSION INFORMATION		
length	beg	30 mins
	int	45 mins
	adv	1hr
type	sprint training	
terrain	flat	
intensity	●●○	●●○　●○○

Spend the first 10 minutes of the session slowly building up to 75% MHR, but don't worry if you don't quite reach that intensity.

Then shift down to a low gear (inside chainring and fairly large sprocket), and pedal as fast as you can for 10 seconds. Recover by shifting up to any gear that feels comfortable and riding at 60–70% MHR for the remainder of a 5-minute period. Repeat this pattern of fast pedaling followed by recovery for the number of times specified. Then complete the session by riding at 60–75% MHR in any gear ratio that you find comfortable. The last few minutes of this, and every other, session should be spent pedaling in a fairly low gear. This helps you to recover from your workout.

Breathing easy
Pedaling fast can make it difficult to maintain rhythmic breathing; place your hands on top of the handlebars, relax your shoulders, and sit upright to open your chest and make breathing easier.

SESSION SUMMARY	Beginner	Intermediate	Advanced
■ Cycle warm-up: Slowly build up to 75% MHR	10 mins	10 mins	10 mins
■ Shift to low gear and spin	10 secs	10 secs	10 secs
■ Cycle at active recovery level (60–70% MHR)	4 mins 50 secs	4 mins 50 secs	4 mins 50 secs
■ Repeat fast pedal/recovery	× 1	× 3	× 5
■ Complete session by cycling at 60–75% MHR	15 mins	20 mins	25 mins
■ Upper body: Lateral raise (*p.56*)	10 reps	15 reps	20 reps
■ Core Exercises (*pp.54–55*)	10 reps	15 reps	20 reps
■ Cool down by stretching (*pp.52–53*)			

TECHNIQUE: SPINNING

The key when spinning is to ensure that only your legs move when you pedal. Keep your hips still and don't allow them to bob up and down so that you are lifted out of the saddle. Focus the power in your legs and feel all the muscles working. Visualize making complete circles with your feet as you pedal. Don't worry if your upper body moves a little at first, spinning fast requires practice and good leg flexibility.

Keep your hips level so that your legs do all the work. If your hips move up and down and you are having to come out of the saddle, shift to a slightly higher gear.

keep shoulders and hips level

> **TIP**
> If you tend to lift out of the saddle when spinning, it may be because you have tight hamstrings. Perform extra leg stretches (see pp.52–53) to increase flexibility in the legs. Check, also, that your saddle height is correct.

other useful techniques setting your riding position pp.30–31   efficient pedaling pp.40–41

WEEK ONE: SESSION THREE

POWER PUSHES

The power push is a dynamic movement that involves pushing hard on the pedals as you pull up on the bike's handlebars. This session will increase leg and upper body strength and provide a strenuous workout, but it won't build bulky muscle.

<table>
<tr><td colspan="3">SESSION INFORMATION</td></tr>
<tr><td>length</td><td>beg</td><td>30 mins</td></tr>
<tr><td></td><td>int</td><td>45 mins</td></tr>
<tr><td></td><td>adv</td><td>1hr</td></tr>
<tr><td>type</td><td colspan="2">sprint training</td></tr>
<tr><td>terrain</td><td colspan="2">flat or slightly rising</td></tr>
<tr><td>intensity</td><td colspan="2">●●● ●●○ ●○○</td></tr>
</table>

Warm up to 75% MHR. Then slow down to almost a stop and perform a power push by shifting to a high gear and pushing hard on the pedals as you pull on the handlebars (*see opposite*). Stay seated in the saddle and try to accelerate as quickly as you can for the time specified. Recover for the remainder of the 5-minute period, then repeat the pattern of hard pedaling followed by recovery for the number of times specified. Finally, finish the session by cycling at 60–70% MHR.

Follow this session either on- or off-road, but perform the pushes on flat or slightly rising terrain. If cycling off-road, soft terrain such as grass adds more resistance and so increases the intensity of the session. If you follow this session on a road, be sure to check for any traffic behind you before each push.

SESSION SUMMARY	Beginner	Intermediate	Advanced
■ Cycle warm-up: Slowly build up to 75% MHR	10 mins	10 mins	10 mins
■ Shift to a high gear and pedal hard, while seated in saddle	10 secs	15 secs	20 secs
■ Cycle at active recovery level (60–75% MHR) in low gear	4 mins 50 secs	4 mins 45 secs	4 mins 40 secs
■ Repeat hard pedal/recovery	× 1	× 2	× 4
■ Complete session by cycling at 60–70% MHR	15 mins	25 mins	30 mins
■ Upper body: Shoulder press (*p.57*)	10 reps	15 reps	20 reps
■ Core Exercises (*pp.54–55*)	10 reps	15 reps	20 reps
■ Cool down by stretching (*pp.52–53*)			

Feel the burn
The muscles in your legs may ache a little as you work hard during the pushes.

TECHNIQUE: POWER PUSHES

It is important to stay in control as you power forward. With practice, you will learn how to shift your weight and use your upper body to balance the powerful pedaling action. Visualize yourself accelerating smoothly, and focus on correct technique for each pedal revolution (*see pp.40–41*).

keep shoulders relaxed

pull up on handlebars

1 Stay seated in the saddle, and shift to a high gear. As you push down on the pedal with your left leg, pull up hard on the handlebars with your left arm and slightly less hard with your right. This brings your torso over to the left and puts your body weight behind the push.

2 Push down on the pedal with your right leg and this time pull up slightly harder on the handlebars with your right arm. Remember to keep your shoulders relaxed. Notice how balancing your arm and body movements helps you to put more power into a push.

other useful techniques safety in traffic pp.44–45 adjusting body position for speed p.87

WEEK ONE: SESSION FOUR

LONG LEISURELY RIDE

This is another stamina-boosting ride designed to increase endurance. The main objective is to ride a little further than you did in Session One, and to enjoy yourself without having rigid instructions to follow. You can ride alone or as part of a group.

SESSION INFORMATION		
length	beg	45 mins
	int	1hr
	adv	1hr 15 mins
type	constant pace	
terrain	flat or undulating	
intensity	●●○ ●●○ ●●○	

Slowly build up to 60% MHR, then ride for the time specified for your fitness level, keeping your heart rate between 60–75% MHR. Use the gear ratios that you feel comfortable with, and vary riding in and out of the saddle on hills. Make the ride more interesting by seeking out more challenging terrains and using the techniques outlined opposite to master them. You might also include some fast-paced bursts, but do not exceed 75% MHR. Try to ride smoothly and remain in control. When you finish this session you should be tired, but not exhausted.

SESSION SUMMARY	Beginner	Intermediate	Advanced
■ Cycle warm-up: Slowly build up to 60% MHR	10 mins	10 mins	10 mins
■ Ride at 60–75% MHR	35 mins	50 mins	65 mins
■ Core Exercises (pp.54–55)	10 reps	15 reps	20 reps
■ Cool down by stretching (pp.52–53)			

INDOOR SESSION ADAPTER

Warm up as specified. Increase resistance/pace until heart rate reaches 75% MHR, then reduce the effort until it falls to 60% MHR. Continue increase/decrease for duration of session. Beginners ride for 40 mins, Intermediate for 50 mins, and Advanced for 60 mins.

Enjoying the scenery
Use your bike to explore; if you are riding a hybrid or a mountain bike, don't confine yourself to the roads.

TECHNIQUE: NEGOTIATING DIFFERENT TERRAINS

On a long ride you might encounter many different terrains. Use this technique to negotiate common terrain variations such as grass and sand. If you come across a terrain that you do not feel confident about riding over, dismount and walk over or around it.

When approaching a patch of grass, hold the handlebars firmly but not too tightly, and relax your shoulders. Lift your butt slightly out of the saddle to keep the bike light, but shift your weight back as you pedal. Grass can be slippery when wet—if it becomes harder to pedal, shift to a lower gear rather than pedaling with more force. You can employ a similar technique to this when approaching a short stretch of sand, only speed up a little beforehand to give you some momentum to plough through.

> ### TIP
> Don't brake or accelerate too hard on wet or loose surfaces; adjust your speed before you reach them. Take care with your steering, too. Cross such surfaces in a straight line. If you do have to steer, make subtle, not extreme, changes in direction.

other useful techniques braking and changing gear *pp.34–35* safety *pp.42–43* tackling an off-road hill *p.115*

WEEK TWO OVERVIEW

This week there is a noticeable contrast between the type of sessions you perform. You learn to use hills to work at increased heart rates, and also to introduce an element of resistance training as you push up them. You also get used to riding your bike at a lower percentage of MHR to help your muscles recover from harder training sessions. For the first time, you train for two days consecutively.

Introducing hills

By Week Two you are ready to work a little harder. Including hills in your sessions is a great way to introduce variety into your rides. You have to work harder to climb them, so your heart rate increases, and you engage more muscles in your arms and legs as you pull on the handlebars and come out of the saddle. You continue to work at stamina-booster level, which increases the amount of oxygen that your muscles receive, but climbing hills and upping your heart rate improves your body's ability to use this oxygen. In "Basic Hills," you push your body to work at a slightly higher intensity (75–80% MHR, or utilization level) for the first time in the Program.

Just as in Week One, there are four sessions to complete this week. Take rest days after Sessions One and Two, but do Sessions Three and Four consecutively. In Session Three the focus is on "active recovery." Working at a low percentage of MHR (60–70%) helps your body to recover from training. The fitter you become, the better your muscles recover if you use them gently between sessions.

Be sure to continue to eat healthily, keep hydrated, and get plenty of sleep as your training becomes more challenging. If you are coping well and don't feel tired, don't be tempted to push yourself beyond what is specified for your fitness level.

Head for the hills
Start incorporating hills into your rides; cycling up them raises your heart rate, then you can recover on the descents.

WEEK TWO AT A GLANCE

Mon	■ Complete rest.
Tues	Session 1: Basic Hills
	■ Interval training.
	■ The core of this session involves riding up hills at utilization level, or 75–80% MHR, then using the descents to recover.
	■ Uphill work that involves pedalling hard and coming out of the saddle increases the resistance training aspect of the session.
Weds	■ Complete rest.
Thur	Session 2: Corner Pushes
	■ Sprint training.
	■ A full-body resistance training session sandwiched between work at stamina-booster level.
Fri	■ Complete rest
Sat	Session 3: Relaxed Spin
	■ Constant pace.
	■ An easy ride at a fairly low percentage of MHR. This has a training benefit because you are burning calories while also helping your body to recover fully in order to cope with the training to come.
Sun	Session 4: Long Ride
	■ Constant pace.
	■ A stamina-booster ride, and your longest so far. Work at this level builds your basic foundation of fitness and prepares you for future hard work.

WEEK TWO: SESSION ONE
BASIC HILLS

Today's session builds fitness by helping to improve the efficiency with which your body uses oxygen. Choose hilly or undulating terrain, and use the climbs to work hard and the descents to recover, so that you follow a basic kind of repeat training.

TECHNIQUE: TACKLING HILLS
Start a climb riding in the saddle, then as you reach the top of the hill, come out of the saddle and pedal hard to maintain your speed. The body positions that you adopt as you climb a hill target many different muscles.

SESSION INFORMATION		
length	beg	30 mins
	int	45 mins
	adv	1hr
type	interval training	
terrain	hilly or undulating	
intensity	●●○ ●●○ ●●○	

stay in the saddle
begin the climb riding in the saddle with your weight well back; hold the handlebars on top and close to the center

crouch down
keep your body low; hold the top of the brake levers and point your elbows out slightly to open your chest and make breathing easier

THE SESSION

Once you have warmed up, ride on undulating terrain at utilization level, or 75–80% MHR, the level at which muscles becomes more efficient at taking up the oxygen that the blood delivers to them. Tackle hills as outlined below. Recover on the descents, using your brakes and your body to control your speed. Finish the session by riding at 60–70% MHR.

SESSION SUMMARY	Beginner	Intermediate	Advanced
■ Cycle warm-up: Build up to then maintain 75% MHR	10 mins	15 mins	15 mins
■ Ride up hills at 75–80% MHR	10 mins	20 mins	30 mins
■ Complete session by riding at 60–70% MHR	10 mins	10 mins	15 mins
■ Core Exercises (pp.54–55)	10 reps	15 reps	20 reps
■ Cool down by stretching (pp.52–53)			

air braking
don't descend too quickly; use your brakes, but help reduce your speed by sitting more upright in the saddle and using your body as an air brake

come out of the saddle
as you reach the top of the hill, get out of the saddle and use all of your body weight to push down hard on the pedals

WEEK TWO: SESSION TWO
CORNER PUSHES

The dynamic movement required to accelerate hard out of a corner builds and strengthens the muscles in your legs. It will also condition the connective tissue that links your muscles and bones and prepare you for more strenuous work later in the Program.

SESSION INFORMATION		
length	beg	30 mins
	int	40 mins
	adv	1hr
type	sprint training	
terrain	flat	
intensity	❤ ●●●	🔧 ●●○ 🏃 ●○○

If possible, choose a fairly flat circuit of track or road, about 1 mile (1.6km) in length, with three or four 90° corners followed by long straights. Warm up to 75% MHR for the time specified, perhaps as part of your ride from home to the circuit. If it is an off-road circuit, take the first corner using the technique outlined opposite. Once your bike is upright, accelerate hard along the straight. Begin out of the saddle, then sit down once you are pedalling quickly. Repeat the corner push/ recovery phase as specified, then finish by cycling at 60–70% MHR.

INDOOR SESSION ADAPTER

Warm up to 75% MHR as specified. Slow until your wheels stop spinning, then all levels accelerate hard for 20 secs. Ride for the remainder of the 2-min period (1min 40 secs) at 60–70% MHR. Repeat stop/accelerate cycle and complete remainder of session as specified below.

TECHNIQUE: RIDING A BERMED CORNER

On off-road terrain, corners often have berms, small trough-like ledges where other vehicles have pushed up the side of the road. Look for berms and use them to help you take corners.

1 As you approach the corner, brake and select the gear (quite a high one) that you are going to use to accelerate out of it. A slow speed is safer, but it also increases the training effect of your acceleration. Look through the corner, and visualize the line you will take.

SESSION SUMMARY	Beginner	Intermediate	Advanced
■ Cycle warm-up: Build up to then maintain 75% MHR	10 mins	15 mins	20 mins
■ Accelerate hard out of corner	20 secs	20 secs	20 secs
■ Ride until next corner at active recovery level (60–70% MHR)	as long as it takes	as long as it takes	as long as it takes
■ Repeat corner accelerations/ recovery	× 4	× 8	× 12
■ Complete session by riding at 60–75% MHR	10 mins	15 mins	20 mins
■ Core Exercises (pp.54–55)	10 reps	15 reps	20 reps
■ Cool down by stretching (pp.52–53)			

2 Keep your inside leg up and lean into the corner, shifting your weight over your outside leg. Aim the bike at the outer wall of the berm, and use it to help you take the corner.

3 Once you have come out of the corner, and the bike is upright, accelerate. Grip the handlebars, come out of the saddle, and pull with both arms as you push with each leg. Take care to look forward, not down.

other useful techniques braking and changing gear *pp.32–33* cornering *pp.36–39*

keep upper
body relaxed

grip handlebars
firmly, but not
too tightly

Taking it easy
A gentle ride can have a regenerating
effect and helps you to recover the
day after a hard training session.

WEEK TWO: SESSION THREE

RELAXED SPIN

The aim of today's ride is to introduce you to exercising at a low level to help you recuperate between more strenuous sessions. As you get fitter, being active on the day following a hard training session helps you to recover from it more quickly than total rest.

SESSION INFORMATION		
length	beg	30 mins
	int	45 mins
	adv	1hr
type	constant pace	
terrain	flat	
intensity	♥ ●○○ ✗✗ ●○○ 🏊 ●○○	

Choose a scenic location such as a public park for this session, but do check beforehand that cycling is permitted.

Build up slowly to 60% MHR, then ride for the time specified for your fitness level, but stay in a low gear and cycle at the active recovery level, or 60–70% MHR.

At this pace, blood flow to your muscles is increased, which provides them with fuel but also has a cleansing and revitalizing effect, since it helps remove waste products that build up during exercise. Try to avoid hills if possible. It is very important not to exceed 70% MHR.

SESSION SUMMARY	Beginner	Intermediate	Advanced
■ Cycle warm-up: Build up slowly to 60% MHR	10 mins	10 mins	10 mins
■ Cycle in a low gear at 60–70% MHR	20 mins	35 mins	50 mins
■ Core Exercises (pp.54–55)	10 reps	15 reps	20 reps
■ Cool down by stretching (pp.52–53)			

TIP
By Week Three, you should be aiming to do this session for 20–30 mins between Program days. It isn't crucial, but you'll find that it helps you to perform better when you train and recover more quickly afterward.

Relaxed riding
On a road bike, it is comfortable to sit quite upright, with your hands on top and toward the middle of the handlebars.

other useful techniques drinking on the move *pp.88–89* riding relaxed *pp.96–97*

WEEK TWO: SESSION FOUR

LONG RIDE

Today you build on your earlier endurance work by taking your longest ride so far. Choose flat or hilly terrain, and ride alone or as part of a group. The key is economy of effort—pace yourself, and learn how to tackle challenges such as hills efficiently.

SESSION INFORMATION		
length	beg	40 mins
	int	1hr 5 mins
	adv	1hr 45 mins
type		constant pace
terrain		flat or hilly
intensity	⬛ ●●●	⬕ ●●○ ⬰ ●●○

Most of this session can be completed on flat roads, but once you have warmed up and reached stamina-booster level, try tackling some hills to make your ride more challenging. Take an energy-efficient approach to hills, and stay within the **70–75% MHR** range, but don't worry if you exceed this for a few seconds. Finish the session by riding at **60–70% MHR**.

SESSION SUMMARY	Beginner	Intermediate	Advanced
▪ Cycle warm-up: Build up to then maintain 60–70% MHR	10 mins	15 mins	20 mins
▪ Cycle mainly at the stamina-booster level (70–75% MHR)	15 mins	30 mins	60 mins
▪ Complete session by riding at 60–70% MHR	15 mins	20 mins	25 mins
▪ Core Exercises (pp.54–55)	10 reps	15 reps	20 reps
▪ Cool down by stretching (pp.52–53)			

INDOOR SESSION ADAPTER
All levels warm up at 60–70% MHR for 10 mins. Then cycle at 70–75% MHR: Beginners ride for 15 mins, Intermediate for 25 mins, and Advanced for 40 mins. Complete remainder of session as specified.

Recover on descents
Having worked hard to climb a hill, relax and take it easy on the way down.

TECHNIQUE: CLIMBING A HILL ECONOMICALLY

A good way to get up a hill quickly is to ride out of the saddle, but that uses a lot of energy. A more efficient approach is to tackle it in a low gear and remain seated in the saddle. Remember to keep your breathing deep and regular, and take care not to push yourself too hard in the early stages.

1 Select a low gear that will allow you to pedal quite quickly. Sit up and hold the outer edges of the handlebars to open your chest and make breathing easier.

hold outer edges of handlebars

2 If the gradient gets steeper and you have no lower gears left, grip the brake hoods and pull on them to help you put more power behind your pedaling. Focus on good pedaling technique: The slower cadences used on a steep climb mean that every part of the pedal revolution helps to power you upward.

grip and pull back on brake hoods

other useful techniques efficient pedaling *pp.40–41*   gear-changing on hills *p.111*

WEEK THREE OVERVIEW

This is the most challenging week so far. Many of you will work at your anaerobic threshold for the first time—that is the hardest you can exercise for an extended period at a constant pace. Although this brings great fitness gains, your body can only maintain this level of exertion for a short time. You must continue to work at lower intensities to support this level of training.

The need for speed

Those following the Program at Intermediate or Advanced level are likely to reach their anaerobic threshold during the first session this week. In "Hard and Easy" you alternate between pushing as hard as you can for 15 seconds and taking the same number of seconds to recover, which will cause your heart rate to steadily rise over the course of the session. Beginners might not reach their anaerobic threshold, but they will still be working hard. This session also provides a good resistance workout, because, as with any type of threshold training, you have to recruit more muscle fibers to push harder in order to increase heart rate.

For the rest of the week you build aerobic fitness further by working more at the stamina-booster and utilization levels.

From this week on, start doing some active recovery between training days. This can be a bike ride such as the "Relaxed Spin" (see pp.80–81), or any other form of light exercise such as walking or swimming. However, don't exceed 70% MHR. If you don't have time to exercise, just try to be more active: Walk more, climb stairs, or do some light stretching (but before stretching, do five minutes of light aerobic exercise beforehand to warm up).

Pushing hard, going fast
Speed is exhilarating, but even if you feel that you are coping well, don't be tempted to exceed session timings.

WEEK THREE AT A GLANCE

Mon
- Active recovery. No session today, but try to be more active than on a regular rest day. Go for an easy 20–30-minute bike ride, swim, or walk.

Tues Session 1: Hard and Easy
- Interval training.
- A challenging aerobic session at a harder level than you've worked at so far.
- Intense periods of effort when accelerating stimulate fast-twitch fibers, helping to tone and shape your muscles.

Weds
- Active recovery, as on Monday.

Thur Session 2: Extended Utilization
- Constant pace.
- Another fairly challenging session with the focus on working hard to build aerobic fitness.

Fri
- Active recovery, as on Monday.

Sat Session 3: Sprints
- Sprint training.
- Some work at the stamina-booster level, with periods of sprinting providing a resistance element, helping to shape and tone.
- A long "warm down" helps prepare you for tomorrow's ride.

Sun Session 4: Group Ride
- Constant pace.
- A long aerobic session, mostly performed at stamina-booster level, but you also push yourself to work harder in places, too.
- Suitable for group riding.

WEEK THREE: SESSION ONE

HARD AND EASY

Great fitness gains can be made by riding at the threshold level, but doing so can produce significant amounts of lactic acid, which has a detrimental effect on your muscles. Here you work close to threshold level, so you reap the benefits but produce no lactic acid.

SESSION INFORMATION		
length	beg	31 mins
	int	42 mins
	adv	48 mins
type	interval training	
terrain	flat, or shallow gradient	
intensity	♥ ●●○	✗ ●●○ ⚐ ●○○

Begin this session by slowly building up to 75% MHR, then maintaining that level for the time specified. Then ride as hard as you can for 15 seconds, followed by riding at an easier pace as you recover for 15 seconds. Adjust your body position accordingly (*see opposite*). Repeat alternating between hard and easy riding for the specified number of times, and as the session continues you should see your heart rate creep up toward your threshold level (80–85% MHR). If you think you might exceed 85% MHR at any point, reduce the effort you make on the next hard part. Finally, finish the session by riding at 60–70% MHR.

While it is easier to control your efforts on flat terrain, you can also follow this session on a shallow gradient. For best results, ride into a headwind to bring extra intensity to the hard parts and so maximize the effects of the session.

Because you are making a series of short, sharp efforts, this session stimulates fast- as well as slow-twitch muscle fibers.

Measured efforts
To get the most out of this session, you really have to push when you ride hard, and relax when you ride easy.

SESSION SUMMARY	Beginner	Intermediate	Advanced
■ Cycle warm-up: Build up to then maintain 75% MHR	15 mins	25 mins	30 mins
■ Ride as hard as you can	15 secs	15 secs	15 secs
■ Ride easy	15 secs	15 secs	15 secs
■ Repeat hard/easy riding	× 4	× 8	× 12
■ Complete session by riding at 60–70% MHR	15 mins	15 mins	15 mins
■ Upper body: Crunch (*p.59*)	10 reps	15 reps	20 reps
■ Core Exercises (*pp.54–55*)	10 reps	15 reps	20 reps
■ Cool down by stretching (*pp.52–53*)			

other useful techniques sprint position p.91 riding in the wind p.129

TECHNIQUE: ADJUSTING BODY POSITION FOR SPEED

Here, your body position changes as you increase your effort. Stay seated in the saddle during the hard pushes, and use your upper body to help your legs accelerate the bike. When you ride easy, adjust your upper body position to allow relaxation and deep breathing.

1 Pedal hard. Push hard on the pedals and pull up on the handlebars; crouch your upper body down, and sit further forward in the saddle to give your arms and legs more power.

2 Pedal easy. Sit up, relax your shoulders and straighten your arms; don't pedal, but don't freewheel: Let your legs turn the pedals without applying power.

WEEK THREE: SESSION TWO

EXTENDED UTILIZATION

Today you build on earlier fitness gains by working again at utilization level. Riding at this level for extended periods requires a great deal of energy, and keeping hydrated is important, so I also demonstrate how to drink while on the move (*see opposite*).

SESSION INFORMATION

length	beg 30 mins
	int 45 mins
	adv 1 hr
type	constant pace
terrain	flat or gently undulating
intensity	●●● ●●○ ●○○

Once you have warmed up to 75% MHR for the time specified, increase your pace and work at 75–80% MHR, or utilization level. Ride on flat or gently undulating terrain for this session, if possible, because it is important to keep your heart rate within the ranges specified. Do not use too high a gear; work hard but stay in control. Anticipate changes in terrain, and make gear shifts before you need to. Finish the session by riding at 60–70% MHR.

Keeping cool
Drink regularly; pouring any excess water over yourself can be refreshing, too.

TECHNIQUE: DRINKING ON THE MOVE ▶

It is important to drink during a strenuous or extended cycling session, even in cold weather. If you don't want to stop—for example, you might want to keep your heart rate within a particular range while training—use this technique to drink safely on the move. Before you venture out onto the road, practice removing the bottle from its holder on the bike.

Note that on a bike with flat handlebars, such as a hybrid or mountain bike, your hands will already be toward the end of the handlebars, so there is no need to adjust their position to help your balance as described in step one.

SESSION SUMMARY	Beginner	Intermediate	Advanced
■ Cycle warm-up: Build up to then maintain 75% MHR	10 mins	15 mins	20 mins
■ Ride at utilization level (75–80% MHR)	10 mins	20 mins	30 mins
■ Complete session by riding at 60–70% MHR	10 mins	10 mins	10 mins
■ Upper body: Biceps curl (*p.57*)	10 reps	15 reps	20 reps
■ Core Exercises (*pp.54–55*)	10 reps	15 reps	20 reps
■ Cool down by stretching (*pp.52–53*)			

TIP
Don't wait until you are thirsty to drink, because by then you will be dehydrated. As you get older, your thirst mechanism becomes less reliable. Try to drink approximately every 10 minutes. Some watches and heart-rate monitors have alarms, which make good reminders.

1 Sit quite upright on your bike. If it feels right to lift your bottle with your right hand, move your left hand towards the top of the left brake lever to counter the change in gravity as you reach down with your right hand.

2 Keep looking forward, and gently pull the bottle from its cage or holder on the bike. Try to keep this movement smooth. Note that you should only attempt this on a flat stretch. Don't drink when cycling up- or downhill.

3 Continue to look forward, put the bottle to your mouth, and tip your head slightly back and to the side. In some cases you may need to use your teeth to pull the cap valve open. Squeeze the bottle and drink, then return it to the cage.

WEEK THREE: SESSION THREE

SPRINTS

This session targets your fast-twitch muscles, and not just in your legs—sprinting is such a dynamic movement that it stimulates muscles all over your body. The efforts you make are short and the recoveries long, but this is the best way to develop pure speed.

SESSION INFORMATION

length	beg	25 mins
	int	45 mins
	adv	1hr 5 mins
type	sprint training	
terrain	flat	
intensity	♥ 🏋 🏃	

Choose a quiet, flat stretch of road for this session. Before each burst of sprinting, remember to look behind you to ensure that the road is clear.

Begin the session by slowly building up to and then holding 75% MHR for the time specified. Then slow down. Next, sprint as hard as you can for 10 seconds. Use what is left of the 5-minute period to recover, cycling at an easy pace, then repeat the sprint/recover drill for the number of times specified.

Resist the tendency to look down during the sprint. Push yourself hard, but stay in control—don't throw your bike from side to side, keep it vertical by pulling up on the handlebars. Finally, finish the session by riding at 60–70% MHR.

SESSION SUMMARY	Beginner	Intermediate	Advanced
■ Cycle warm-up: Build up to then maintain 75% MHR	10 mins	15 mins	20 mins
■ Sprint	10 secs	10 secs	10 secs
■ Ride at active recovery level (60–65% MHR)	4 mins 50 secs	4 mins 50 secs	4 mins 50 secs
■ Repeat sprint/recovery	× 1	× 3	× 5
■ Complete session by riding at 60–70% MHR	10 mins	15 mins	20 mins
■ Core Exercises (*pp.54–55*)	10 reps	15 reps	20 reps
■ Cool down by stretching (*pp.52–53*)			

use hips to drive leg down

Sprinting out of the saddle
Get out of the saddle and push down hard with each pedal effort as you pull up on the handlebars to keep the bike vertical.

TECHNIQUE: SPRINT POSITION

With correct sprinting technique, your entire body gets a good workout, not just your legs. Good technique will also ensure that you sprint in a straight line, which is most important for safety.

Keep your chest and torso parallel with the ground and your back as flat as possible. Pull upward on the handlebars to help you control the bike and keep it vertical.

pull up equally on the handlebars

other useful techniques sprint-pedaling uphill *p.99* standing starts *pp.108–109*

WEEK THREE: SESSION FOUR
GROUP RIDE

Today the goal is to cycle at a comfortable pace but for longer than you have done so far in the Program. This will help to build endurance. Try riding with friends or family to make the session more fun; that way you can share the lead and the experience.

SESSION INFORMATION		
length	beg	1hr 10 mins
	int	1hr 25 mins+
	adv	1hr 40 mins+
type	constant pace	
terrain	undulating	
intensity	❤ ●●●	🍴 ●●○	🏃 ●●○

Enjoy this long ride, and work hard, but remember to keep to a comfortable pace. In order to build endurance, today's session must be totally aerobic—needing to take deep breaths after speaking is a sign that you are working at the correct level—but do not exceed 80% MHR. However, the session will also be less effective if your heart rate drops below 60% MHR, which might be the case if you are cycling with your family or have small children to consider. One way to increase the work is to carry extra weight.

SESSION SUMMARY	Beginner	Intermediate	Advanced
■ Cycle warm-up: Slowly build up to 75% MHR	10 mins	10 mins	10 mins
■ Ride at any pace that feels comfortable, but do not exceed 80% MHR	1 hour	1 hour 15 mins to 1 hour 30 mins	1 hour 30 mins to 1 hour 45 mins
■ Core Exercises (*pp.54–55*)	10 reps	15 reps	20 reps
■ Cool down by stretching (*pp.52–53*)			

INDOOR SESSION ADAPTER

Warm up as specified. All levels increase resistance/pace until heart rate reaches 80% MHR, then reduce effort until it falls to 70%. Continue increase/decrease for duration of session. Beginners ride for 20 mins, Intermediate for 30 mins, and Advanced for 40 mins.

Working harder
Make the ride more challenging by carrying weight, such as a picnic in a backpack or a child in a child's seat.

other useful techniques riding relaxed *pp.96–97* overtaking *pp.118–119*

TECHNIQUE: KEEPING A SAFE DISTANCE

Riding with a group is great fun and can be inspiring, but there is always the danger of running into another group member, especially on off-road single tracks where you are following each other. On the road, always remember to ride in single file when being overtaken by traffic.

Take care to keep your distance when following each other, especially on descents. You cannot see what lies ahead and if the rider in front suddenly slows, you need to allow enough space to brake safely. Keep a safe distance from the rider in front by looking at his or her shoulders, not the rear wheel of their bike.

WEEK FOUR OVERVIEW

You are now halfway through the Program. Your base level of aerobic fitness should have improved, and you are probably noticing that your muscles are becoming more toned and shapely. One way to measure your progress is to repeat the Bike Test (*see p.63*) that you did at the start of the Program. Although there are sessions that target and tone your muscles this week, the focus is on the test.

Testing and measuring progress

This week consists of three sessions and a bike test. The test measures just one aspect of your improved fitness—your ability to ride your bike at speed. Being able to ride your bike more quickly than at the start of the Program is a good guide to improvement, but it isn't the only one. How you feel, and your fitter and firmer body are both better. Don't worry if you can't beat your earlier time. Often people don't begin to see results until after five weeks. And factors beyond your control can affect your performance too, for example weather conditions, mood, and general health. Stay focused, continue with the Program, and you will soon see improvement.

To prepare yourself for the test, Session One is the "Rejuvenation Ride." It is similar to the "Relaxed Spin" that you did during Week Two, and to the active recovery rides that you may have been completing between training sessions. The "Rejuvenation Ride" includes some fast efforts to help prepare you for the test. In between Sessions One and Two, do the Bike Test. Then there are two more sessions to complete this week. "Hill Sprints" provides a good whole-body resistance workout, and the "Adventure Ride" will continue to develop your aerobic fitness.

Beating your time
Monitor improvements in your fitness level by doing a time test—the results can be an excellent motivator to work harder.

WEEK FOUR AT A GLANCE

Mon
- Active recovery. Go for an easy 20–30-minute bike ride in low gears, or do any other form of light exercise.

Tues Session 1: Rejuvenation Ride
- Interval training.
- A ride at a fairly low MHR, but with some bursts of harder work to prepare you for the test the following day.

Weds The Bike Test
- Constant pace.
- Measure your progress by going back and repeating the Bike Test (see p.63).

Thur
- Active recovery, as on Monday.

Fri
- Active recovery, as on Monday.

Sat Session 2: Hill Sprints
- Sprint training.
- Some work at the stamina-booster level, with harder efforts required during the sprints.
- Long active-recovery periods between sprints ensure that muscles benefit from the full toning and shaping effects of the session.

Sun Session 3: Adventure Ride
- Constant pace.
- Suitable for group riding.
- Some work at the stamina-booster level, then working up to utilization to prepare you for more advanced work in the weeks to come.

WEEK FOUR: SESSION ONE

REJUVENATION

The aim of this session is to prepare you for tomorrow's test. By now you may be finding that you feel better if you factor active recovery into the Program between training days, rather than having a day of complete rest. This is active recovery with a twist.

Warm up at the start of this session by riding in a low gear for 10 minutes, keeping your heart rate between 60–70% MHR. Then, in the same low gear, pedal quickly for 30 seconds, building up the speed with which you pedal, so that by the end you are really working hard and pedaling as fast as you are able. During this effort, keep your upper body relaxed and don't be tempted to come out of the saddle. Recover for 4 minutes, then repeat the fast pedaling/recovery phase for the number of times specified. Finally, finish the session by riding at a steady 60–70% MHR.

Think of your body as being like a car—it works best if it is driven every day, but not at low engine revs. In this session, when you make your fast-pedaling effort, you are revving your engine in preparation for giving it full throttle tomorrow. For the rest of the session, you ride relaxed (*see opposite*). Remember, before moving onto Session Two, complete the Bike Test (*see p.63*).

SESSION INFORMATION

length	beg	29 mins
	int	33 mins 30 secs
	adv	38 mins
type	interval training	
terrain	flat or undulating	
intensity	●●○ ●●● ●●○	

TECHNIQUE: RIDING RELAXED ▶

On flat or gently uphill terrain with little or no traffic around, you will be accustomed to riding your bike in a fairly upright position and supporting yourself with almost straight arms. It is important to maintain this easy posture, with shoulders relaxed, whenever you ride. Focus on your head and neck area, since there can be a tendency for tension to build up there when riding.

When cycling up a slight gradient or on a descent, you need to make slight adjustments to your hand and body positions to ensure that you stay safe and in control.

SESSION SUMMARY	Beginner	Intermediate	Advanced
■ Cycle warm-up: Ride at 60–70% MHR in a low gear	10 mins	10 mins	10 mins
■ Pedal quickly in a low gear	30 secs	30 secs	30 secs
■ Ride at active recovery level (60–65% MHR)	4 mins	4 mins	4 mins
■ Repeat quick pedal/recovery	× 2	× 3	× 4
■ Complete session by riding at 60–70% MHR	10 mins	10 mins	10 mins
■ Core Exercises (*pp.54–55*)	10 reps	15 reps	20 reps
■ Cool down by stretching (*pp.52–53*)			

TIP

Stretch your hamstrings (at the backs of your thighs) when riding by rising from the saddle with pedals parallel to the ground and straightening your legs. Then sit down again.

bend your
arms to absorb
road shock

keep arms
straight when
you brake

When cycling on a slight gradient, hold the tops of the brake levers on a road bike. This will allow you to pull on the handlebars, which increases the power that you can put behind your pedaling. This is also the best position when riding in traffic, because your hands are closer to the brakes.

On descents it is best to keep your center of gravity as low as possible as this makes the bike more stable. Hold the bottom of the handlebars and position your hands over the brake levers to give you the maximum pull on them—the faster you go, the more force you need to apply to the brakes to slow down.

other useful techniques braking and changing gear *pp.32–35* spinning *p.69*

WEEK FOUR: SESSION TWO

HILL SPRINTS

This is sprinting but with the added challenge of riding uphill. The session targets all the muscles of the body, but it really gives the legs a strenuous workout. As usual, correct technique is important—you need to adjust your foot position slightly when sprinting uphill.

SESSION INFORMATION

length	beg	25 mins
	int	45 mins
	adv	1hr 5 mins
type	sprint training	
terrain	hilly	
intensity	●●○	●●● ●●●

Choose a short, fairly steep hill, either on- or off-road. If you perform this session on a road, choose one with very little traffic.

Begin by slowly building up to and then holding 75% MHR. Then select a hill and sprint up it as hard as you can for 10 seconds. Get out of the saddle, and be sure to maintain good pedaling technique (*see opposite*). Do not sprint so hard that you cannot ride in a straight line. Recover for what remains of a 5-minute period by cycling on flat terrain. Then repeat the sprint/recovery phase for the number of times specified. Finally, finish by riding at 60–70% MHR.

One key to fitness progression is to continuously challenge your muscles to work in different ways. Combining sprinting with uphill work targets the fast-twitch fibers and will help to shape and tone your entire body.

Accelerating smoothly
Pull hard on the handlebars, and point your toes as you pull back and up on the pedals.

SESSION SUMMARY	Beginner	Intermediate	Advanced
■ Cycle warm-up: Build up to then maintain 75% MHR	10 mins	15 mins	20 mins
■ On an up-slope, sprint	10 secs	10 secs	10 secs
■ Ride at active recovery level (60–65% MHR)	4 mins 50 secs	4 mins 50 secs	4 mins 50 secs
■ Repeat sprint/recovery	× 1	× 3	× 5
■ Complete session by riding at 60–70% MHR	10 mins	15 mins	20 mins
■ Core Exercises (*pp.54–55*)	10 reps	15 reps	20 reps
■ Cool down by stretching (*pp.52–53*)			

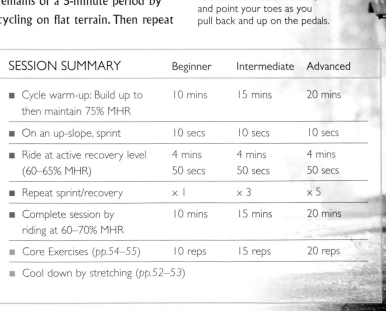

TECHNIQUE: SPRINT-PEDALING UPHILL

When making an out-of-the-saddle effort to sprint uphill, exaggerate the standard pedaling motion in order to get every bit of power from your body into the pedals.

1 As you push down on the pedal, drop your heel slightly. This will give you greater range of movement in the next phase, and means you can apply more force to the pedal.

2 When climbing out of the saddle, pull back and upward with your foot. Try not to claw backward at the bottom of the pedal stroke.

3 Pull upward on the pedal in the recovery phase. Your body is in front of the pedal and it should feel as if you are pulling it after you. Feel your hamstrings working.

other useful techniques efficient pedaling *pp.40–41* sprint position *p.91*

WEEK FOUR: SESSION THREE

ADVENTURE RIDE

The aim of today's session is to cycle for longer than you have done before. Make the ride more interesting by incorporating an element of adventure into it. Plan a new route, or take your bike by vehicle, and cycle in a different area. Try riding off-road on different terrain.

SESSION INFORMATION		
length	beg	1hr 10 mins
	int	1hr 40 mins
	adv	1hr 55 mins
type	constant pace	
terrain	undulating	
intensity	●●● ●●○ ●○○	

Follow this session with a group or on your own. The aim is just to ride for the time specified. Generally, do not exceed 80% MHR, but doing so on the occasional hill will not hurt at this stage of the Program—it will stimulate your fast-twitch muscles, and because you are fitter now, you won't have any problem coping with the extra effort. However, if you feel good, don't push yourself to work harder, just ride for longer.

SESSION SUMMARY	Beginner	Intermediate	Advanced
■ Cycle warm-up: Slowly build up to 70% MHR	10 mins	10 mins	10 mins
■ Ride at any comfortable pace not exceeding 80% MHR	at least 1 hour	at least 1 hour 30 mins	at least 1 hour 45 mins
■ Core Exercises (pp.54–55)	10 reps	15 reps	20 reps
■ Cool down by stretching (pp.52–53)			

INDOOR SESSION ADAPTER

Warm up as specified. Ride at a constant pace, keeping between 70–80% MHR. Beginners ride for 40 mins, Intermediate for 50 mins, and Advanced for 60 mins.

TECHNIQUE: NEGOTIATING A DROP-OFF

Abrupt changes of gradient, step-like drops, and roots are all common features of off-road trails, but with this technique you won't have to dismount and tackle difficult terrain on foot, you can ride over and continue with your training. Approach slowly, and control the bike with your arms and shoulders. Note that this technique is only suitable for tackling small drop-offs of no more than about 1ft (30cm) in height.

1 Slow down as you approach the drop-off, and select the point at which you are going to cross it. Line up your bike with that point, come out of the saddle and prepare yourself for the drop-off.

2 Pedal the bike forward, and just as your front wheel crosses the lip of the drop-off, pull up on the handlebars. As you do this, move your weight backward to unload the front wheel.

3 Keep your weight back until the front wheel lands below the drop-off, but as soon as it does shift your weight forward so that the back wheel is unloaded when it lands. Pedal forward once both wheels are on the ground, then continue with your ride.

TIP
Before you cross a drop-off, take a moment to line up your route away from it. This will prevent hesitation about which way to go once you have negotiated the drop-off. On very rough terrain, ride slowly at first to give yourself time to pick a line, then continue at a pace at which you feel in control.

other useful techniques braking and changing gear off-road *pp.34–35* negotiating obstacles *p.121*

WEEK FIVE OVERVIEW

In Week Five you do more work at your anaerobic threshold, the level where great fitness gains are made. You are ready for more challenges now that you have developed your broad base of aerobic fitness. At this point in the Program, I introduce more sessions where you accelerate to near your anaerobic threshold level and then back off. This introduces a resistance element to the workouts.

Going faster, getting stronger

Session One is "Flat Threshold Repeats" where you ride at your anaerobic threshold heart rate for a sustained period of time and then repeat the efforts. This is a challenging session, but by now you are fit enough to handle it.

During "Ins and Outs" you accelerate up to your threshold level, decelerate and then accelerate again. This provides a good resistance workout as well as an aerobic one. You will notice these methods of training combined in future sessions. All threshold work, although principally aerobic training, has resistance training benefits simply because you must push harder on the pedals to do it.

During this week you continue to develop your base level of fitness as each session involves work at stamina-booster intensity. In "Standing Starts" you combine resistance and aerobic work again. By now you should be noticing that your muscles are stronger, firmer, and more toned.

This is a challenging week, and you may be discovering that training can be mentally as well as physically demanding. If you feel very tired, rest on Friday. You always recover better physically by doing light exercise between session days, but sometimes it is mentally easier to cope with a training regime if you can stand back from it for a day.

Pushing hard
Training at anaerobic threshold level boosts aerobic fitness, but it provides an excellent resistance workout, too.

WEEK FIVE AT A GLANCE	
Mon	■ Active recovery. Go for an easy 20–30-minute bike ride, or do some other physical activity. Do no exceed 70% MHR, and spend most of your session below that level.
Tues	Session 1: Flat Threshold Repeats ■ Interval training. ■ Longer efforts than you have been used to, and at the more challenging threshold level.
Weds	■ Active recovery, as on Monday.
Thurs	Session 2: Ins and Outs ■ Interval training. ■ Some work at the stamina-booster level, then extra bursts of effort at threshold level. ■ Periods of hard work when accelerating to threshold level add a resistance training element to the session.
Fri	■ Active recovery, as on Monday. ■ If you feel very tired, have a day off and do no physical exercise.
Sat	Session 3: Standing Starts ■ Sprint training. ■ Part of the ride at stamina-booster level, then resistance work achieved by repeatedly slowing down and then accelerating.
Sun	Session 4: Utilization Repeats ■ Interval training. ■ More work at the stamina-booster and utilization levels. ■ Hard work, but with your increased level of fitness you should enjoy this session.

WEEK FIVE: SESSION ONE

FLAT THRESHOLD REPEATS

This is a tough session, but by now you are fit enough to handle it. Choose any terrain, but during the threshold intervals you need to keep your effort constant, so here I outline a technique for handling hazards such as changing road surfaces that may slow your pace.

SESSION INFORMATION		
length	beg	30 mins
	int	45 mins
	adv	1hr
type	interval training	
terrain	flat or undulating	
intensity	♥♥♥ 🚴♦♦♦ 🏃♦♦○	

Begin the session by riding for the time specified, slowly building up to and then maintaining 75% MHR. Then increase your effort and ride at threshold level (80–85% MHR) for the time specified. Recover by riding at a more relaxed pace of 60–70% MHR for the same amount of time. Repeat this cycle of threshold-level effort followed by recovery-pace riding twice. Finish the session by riding for the period specified at 60–70% MHR in a lower gear than you would normally use.

When you work at maximum effort during the threshold periods, your body might begin to produce lactic acid, but to progress with the Program, you have to get it used to processing this waste product. Pedaling quite quickly against a light resistance, as you do in the last stage of the session, is a good way of flushing lactic acid out of your system.

TECHNIQUE: NEGOTIATING HAZARDS

Whether you ride on- or off-road it is quite likely that you will encounter loose and uneven surfaces such as cobblestones, gravel, and sand. You can ride over these terrains safely, and without losing much speed, by following this technique.

SESSION SUMMARY	Beginner	Intermediate	Advanced
■ Cycle warm-up: Build up to then maintain 75% MHR	10 mins	15 mins	20 mins
■ Ride at threshold level (80–85% MHR)	2 mins	4 mins	6 mins
■ Ride at active recovery level (60–70% MHR)	2 mins	4 mins	6 mins
■ Repeat threshold/recovery	× 2	× 2	× 2
■ Complete session by riding at 60–70% MHR	12 mins	14 mins	16 mins
■ Upper body: Biceps curl (p.57)	10 reps	15 reps	20 reps
■ Core Exercises (pp.54–55)	10 reps	15 reps	20 reps
■ Cool down by stretching (pp.52–53)			

1 When cycling hard over flat, even terrain, push with your legs as you pull up on the handlebars. Keep your weight evenly distributed between the front and rear of the bike.

move body weight
over rear wheel to
help traction

2 If you encounter a stretch of loose or uneven surface such as cobblestones, don't panic and brake suddenly as this will probably cause the bike to slip from under you. Instead, simply sit further back in the saddle, which will help to give your rear wheel extra grip or traction, and power through. Hold the handlebars firmly but not too tightly.

other useful techniques negotiating different terrains p.73 drinking on the move p.88–89

WEEK FIVE: SESSION TWO

INS AND OUTS

This is another threshold session, but because Session One this week was so demanding, today you work hard for less time. You ride at the threshold level for long enough to benefit but not long enough to produce large quantities of lactic acid, which can damage muscles.

SESSION INFORMATION

length	beg	26 mins
	int	37 mins
	adv	52 mins
type	interval training	
terrain	undulating	
intensity	●●●	●●● ●●○

If you follow this session off-road, you could use a series of short, steep hills, making efforts on the ascents and recovering on the down-slopes.

Over the time specified, warm up by building up to and then holding 75% MHR. Then increase your pace to 80% MHR and work at that level for 5 seconds. Then reduce your effort until your heart rate drops to 70% MHR, and maintain that pace for 5 seconds.

Repeat this process of increasing your pace and working hard for 5 seconds, then easing off for the specified number of times. Each time you pick up the pace, push extra hard for the first five pedal revolutions. These frequent changes of pace provide a rigorous aerobic workout and will also help to stimulate your fast-twitch muscles, which will shape and tone your legs. Complete the session by riding for the specified time at 60–75% MHR.

TECHNIQUE: NEGOTIATING UNEVEN TERRAIN ▶

When riding off-road, traction is important, particularly when tackling hills. Use this technique to keep your wheels in contact with the trail, so that you are always in control of your bike—and safe.

On off-road descents, it is best to get out of the saddle and let the bike move underneath you. Flex your arms and legs slightly, but keep your body relaxed so that the bike absorbs any bumps from the uneven terrain. The steeper the descent, the further back you should shift your weight. Be sure to look forward.

SESSION SUMMARY	Beginner	Intermediate	Advanced
■ Cycle warm-up: Build up to then maintain 75% MHR	10 mins	15 mins	20 mins
■ Increase pace to 80% MHR	5 secs at 80%	5 secs at 80%	5 secs at 80%
■ Ease off until heart rate falls to 70% MHR	5 secs at 70%	5 secs at 70%	5 secs at 70%
■ Repeat pace increase/decrease	× 2	× 4	× 8
■ Complete session by riding at 60–75% MHR	12 mins	14 mins	16 mins
■ Upper body: Lateral raise (p.56)	10 reps	15 reps	20 reps
■ Core Exercises (pp.54–55)	10 reps	15 reps	20 reps
■ Cool down by stretching (pp.52–53)			

TIP

Think about your arms and legs acting as your body's suspension system—they flex at the elbows and knees and act as shock absorbers. As they soak up bumps from the trail, they are also getting a good workout.

other useful techniques negotiating a drop-off p.101 negotiating obstacles p.121

WEEK FIVE: SESSION THREE

STANDING STARTS

This session involves sprinting, so it targets fast-twitch muscles, but because you accelerate from almost a standstill, you will need to use more muscle power than when sprinting uphill. You sprint for longer in this session, and as a result really build aerobic fitness.

SESSION INFORMATION

length	beg	25 mins
	int	43 mins
	adv	63 mins
type	sprint training	
terrain	flat	
intensity	♥ ●●○	🏋 ●●●	🏃 ●●○

Warm up to 75% MHR for the time specified. Then shift to a gear ratio with the chain on the biggest chainring and a mid-sized sprocket, and on a flat stretch of road, slow almost to a stop. Check behind for traffic, and then perform a standing start (*see opposite*) by getting out of the saddle and accelerating, pushing hard on the pedals with all your strength. Concentrate on keeping your bike straight during your initial effort. Once you are pedaling quite quickly, sit in the saddle and continue for the rest of the 20 seconds. Recover for 2 minutes, then pedal lightly for a further 15 seconds. Repeat the acceleration/recovery process as specified.

Finish by cycling at 60–70% MHR for the time specified, but use a lower gear than normal to help your legs recover more quickly.

Power and control
Don't look at the ground; pull up on the handlebars with your weight well forward.

SESSION SUMMARY	Beginner	Intermediate	Advanced
■ Cycle warm-up: Build up to then maintain 75% MHR	10 mins	15 mins	20 mins
■ Slow to walking pace, then accelerate as fast as you can	20 secs	20 secs	20 secs
■ Ride at active recovery level (60–70%)	2 mins	2 mins	2 mins
■ Pedal light for 15 seconds	15 secs	15 secs	15 secs
■ Repeat acceleration/recovery	× 2	× 3	× 5
■ Complete session by riding at 60–70% MHR	10 mins	20 mins	30 mins
■ Core Exercises (*pp.54–55*)	10 reps	15 reps	20 reps
■ Cool down by stretching (*pp.52–53*)			

TECHNIQUE: STANDING STARTS

Correct technique is essential for you to get the most benefit from this session but it is also very important for safety. Starting from a slow speed can cause you to wobble: On-road this can bring you into the path of traffic, and off-road it could cause you to lose traction and fall. Whether you perform standing starts on- or off-road, be sure to look behind you and check that you are not about to be overtaken before you accelerate.

1 Look behind and check that the road or trail is clear. If your bike has dropped handlebars, hold the top of them as you turn your head. Be careful not to pull them in the direction you are looking, as this will cause the bike to swerve.

2 Hold the bottom of the handlebars to give you maximum leverage. Push down hard with your left leg, pull up with your right, and pull on the handlebars to assist your legs. Pull up equally on both sides of the handlebars.

3 Push down hard with your right leg as you pull up with your left. Pedal until your legs are moving too quickly to remain comfortably out of the saddle. If this takes more than 20 seconds, shift to a lower gear for the next start.

other useful techniques braking and changing gear *pp.32–35* safety in traffic *pp.44–45*

WEEK FIVE: SESSION FOUR

UTILIZATION REPEATS

Riding for extended periods at utilization level develops aerobic fitness, however it also requires a lot of energy. Here you ride for longer than you have done before at this level, but the session is divided into segments so you have time to recover between efforts.

SESSION INFORMATION		
length	beg	1hr
	int	1hr 20 mins
	adv	1hr 40 mins
type	interval training	
terrain	undulating or hilly	
intensity	♥ ●●●	⚡ ●●○ 🏃 ●●○

Follow this session on undulating or even hilly terrain. Avoid big, very steep hills, but smaller ones will not hurt, especially if you use the technique outlined opposite to keep your heart rate within the specified ranges. Begin by warming up to, then holding **75% MHR**. Then ride for the time specified at **75–80% MHR**, utilization level, and recover by riding for the same time at **60–70% MHR**. Repeat this effort/ recovery cycle three times. Finish by riding at **60–70% MHR**.

SESSION SUMMARY	Beginner	Intermediate	Advanced
■ Cycle warm-up: Build up to then maintain 75% MHR	10 mins	15 mins	20 mins
■ Ride at utilization level (75–80% MHR)	5 mins	10 mins	15 mins
■ Ride at 60–70% MHR	5 mins	5 mins	5 mins
■ Repeat utilization/recovery	× 3	× 3	× 3
■ Complete session by riding at 60–70% MHR	20 mins	20 mins	20 mins
■ Upper body: Lateral raise (p.56)	10 reps	15 reps	20 reps
■ Core Exercises (pp.54–55)	10 reps	15 reps	20 reps
■ Cool down by stretching (pp.52–53)			

INDOOR SESSION ADAPTER

All levels take 10 mins to build up to 75% MHR. Ride at 75–80% MHR as specified, then recover by riding at 60–70% MHR for 5 mins. All levels repeat twice. Then all levels complete session by riding at 60–70% MHR for 10 mins.

Tackle hills conservatively
Small hills won't pose a problem if you use good technique to climb them.

TECHNIQUE: GEAR-CHANGING ON HILLS

It takes practice to master the skill of shifting gears to control your effort on undulating or hilly terrain. Use low gears for uphill and high gears for down. Look ahead and shift gears in advance of a change in terrain.

1 Shift gears well before a change in gradient. For climbing hills, you need lower gears: The smaller the chainring and larger the sprocket, the lower the gear. If the gear shift lever is incorporated in your brake levers, ride with your hands on top of them for easy access.

2 On a hill, there may be many changes of gradient on one climb, and you may need to shift gear more than once to accommodate them. Be sure to shift before the steeper or shallower stretch arrives to keep your effort more constant.

keep back straight

3 Come out of the saddle, and use your body weight to help you tackle steep gradients economically. Pull on each side of the handlebars, and shift your body in time with your legs. Keep your back straight and your chest open so you do not constrict your breathing.

other useful techniques braking and changing gear *pp.32–35* tackling hills *pp.76–77*

WEEK SIX OVERVIEW

You head into the hills again this week—there is no better place for high-intensity work. Hills provide a good aerobic workout, and because you have to push hard on the pedals to get up them, you also target your muscles with resistance training. Seek out some undulating terrain as at least two sessions this week involve hill work. You also learn a new way to train with friends.

Meeting new challenges

Your first session this week is "Hill Threshold Repeats." This provides a good aerobic workout and also targets the muscles in your legs. In this session I recommend coming out of the saddle as you climb, which will also exercise your upper body. Take care with this session. If your heart rate does not reach your threshold range after the first repeat, ease off and complete the session by riding at 60–70% MHR. Consider going back and repeating Week Five from Session Two onward. Then try Week Six again.

The five weeks of the Program that you have completed so far should have prepared you for "Deep Muscle Repeats." You need to be fit, but your tendons and ligaments have to be strong, too. You should really feel your legs having to work hard in this session. Because you use a lot of muscle fibers, be sure to keep your legs warm. If it's a cold day, keep your legs covered (see pp.22–25).

In "Group Repeats," you can involve friends in your training session. You learn how to follow at a safe distance and to overtake, but do take care to stay away from busy roads.

Finally, "Utilization Ride" is a taxing workout. But by this point in the Program your increased level of fitness means you enjoy challenges like this.

Tackling hills
Hills are great for bike workouts; start in a low gear, and begin conservatively to avoid tiring yourself out early on.

WEEK SIX AT A GLANCE

Mon ■ Active recovery. This should be a regular part of your training schedule by now. Practice any light exercise that you enjoy.

Tues Session 1: Hill Threshold Repeats
■ Interval training.
■ A challenging session in which you use hills to work at threshold level and then recover.

Weds ■ Active recovery, as on Monday.

Thurs Session 2: Deep Muscle Repeats
■ Interval training.
■ Hard work in a high gear provides an excellent toning and strengthening training session for your legs.
■ Work at stamina-booster level helps maintain your improved level of aerobic fitness.

Fri ■ Active recovery, as on Monday.

Sat Session 3: Group Repeats
■ Interval training.
■ If possible, this session should be followed in a group of three.
■ Riders alternate leading the group and working at utilization level for short periods.

Sun Session 4: Utilization Ride
■ Constant pace.
■ A fairly hard ride at utilization level, with periods of recovery on hill descents.

WEEK SIX: SESSION ONE

HILL THRESHOLD REPEATS

You will be working at threshold level again today, but because the repeats are uphill you'll need to apply more force to the pedals and, as a result, use more muscle fibers. Try to ride part of the hill out of the saddle to ensure that your upper body gets a good workout too.

<table>
<tr><td colspan="3">SESSION INFORMATION</td></tr>
<tr><td>length</td><td>beg</td><td>31 mins</td></tr>
<tr><td></td><td>int</td><td>44 mins</td></tr>
<tr><td></td><td>adv</td><td>1hr 2 mins</td></tr>
<tr><td>type</td><td colspan="2">interval training</td></tr>
<tr><td>terrain</td><td colspan="2">hilly</td></tr>
<tr><td>intensity</td><td colspan="2"> </td></tr>
</table>

Find a hill that takes you about 4 minutes to climb, preferably one that gets steeper toward the top. If you do this session off-road, use the technique outlined opposite for climbing hills economically.

Begin the session by slowly warming up to 75% MHR. Then ride uphill at 80–85% MHR, shifting gears to keep you within the heart rate range specified. If you can, ride for the last 30 seconds out of the saddle at exactly 85% MHR. Recover by riding downhill and on the flat before it, then repeat the hill climb/recovery phase the specified number of times. End the session by riding at 60–70% MHR.

Whenever you ride a session involving hills, think of the word "light"; visualize yourself being light and your bike having no weight on the ground. You'll be surprised by how effective this is.

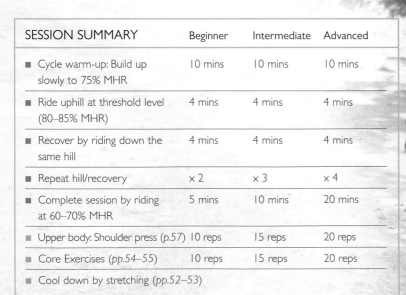

SESSION SUMMARY	Beginner	Intermediate	Advanced
■ Cycle warm-up: Build up slowly to 75% MHR	10 mins	10 mins	10 mins
■ Ride uphill at threshold level (80–85% MHR)	4 mins	4 mins	4 mins
■ Recover by riding down the same hill	4 mins	4 mins	4 mins
■ Repeat hill/recovery	× 2	× 3	× 4
■ Complete session by riding at 60–70% MHR	5 mins	10 mins	20 mins
■ Upper body: Shoulder press (p.57)	10 reps	15 reps	20 reps
■ Core Exercises (pp.54–55)	10 reps	15 reps	20 reps
■ Cool down by stretching (pp.52–53)			

Hill work
Don't throw your bike from side to side, keep it vertical; maintain control by pulling back on the handlebars.

TECHNIQUE: TACKLING AN OFF-ROAD HILL

Climbing the steep part of an off-road hill requires a slightly different technique to on-road. For the latter, you get out of the saddle, shift your weight forward, and almost push and pull your bike up after you. If you do that on trails and loose terrain, you could lose traction and cause the rear wheel to spin, which might mean a fall.

1 As the gradient gets steeper, shift gear, and when you have no gears left, move forward in the saddle but pull back on the handlebars. It is important to keep as much weight as possible back over the rear wheel to help traction.

2 If the hill becomes very steep, come out of the saddle to help power you forward. Remember to keep your weight back and your body low—the key is to hover over the saddle. Continue to pull back on the handlebars, not up.

other useful techniques braking and changing gear off-road *pp.34–35* negotiating hazards *pp.104–105*

WEEK SIX: SESSION TWO

DEEP MUSCLE REPEATS

This session is like weight-training on a bike. Here you ride in a high gear and push very hard on the pedals so that your fast-twitch muscles are stimulated. This is a tough session; be sensible about how hard you push yourself, and maintain good technique throughout.

SESSION INFORMATION

length	beg	31 mins
	int	44 mins
	adv	57 mins
type	interval training	
terrain	flat	
intensity		

Begin by riding for the time specified, building up to and then maintaining 75% MHR. Then, on a flat or slightly rising section of road or trail, shift to a high gear and pedal hard for 1 minute. Choose a gear ratio that means you do not pedal at more than 60 revolutions per minute. Count your revolutions for 10 seconds to check this. Keep your upper body still. Power with your legs, and concentrate on maintaining good pedaling technique. Recover by riding for 2 minutes at a lower heart rate, and repeat riding hard and then recovering for the number of times specified. Finally, end the session by riding at 60–75% MHR. If you have coped well and feel good, aim to stay closer to 75% than to 60% MHR.

This session does put some strain on your muscle and bone connective tissue, but you should be able to handle it by now. However, if you experience pain in your legs, knees, or back, stop immediately. Ride home in a low gear, and seek medical advice before you continue.

TECHNIQUE: PEDALING IN A HIGH GEAR ▶

When pedaling in a high gear, correct technique is essential to get the most from every part of the revolution and ensure that as many muscle fibers as possible are recruited. Focus on keeping your shoulders and hips still in order to help isolate your legs—they should do all the work.

Brace your upper body and keep it still by holding the handlebars firmly. You should aim to keep your shoulders and hips as level as possible and your legs will then power you forward.

SESSION SUMMARY	Beginner	Intermediate	Advanced
■ Cycle warm-up: Build up to then maintain 75% MHR	10 mins	15 mins	20 mins
■ Shift to high gear and ride hard	1 min	1 min	1 min
■ Ride at 60–70% MHR	2 mins	2 mins	2 mins
■ Repeat	× 2	× 3	× 4
■ Complete session by riding at 60–75% MHR	15 mins	20 mins	25 mins
■ Upper body: Biceps curl (p.57)	10 reps	15 reps	20 reps
■ Core Exercises (pp.54–55)	10 reps	15 reps	20 reps
■ Cool down by stretching (pp.52–53)			

TIP
Use this session to target your core muscles (see pp.10–11). During the repeats, tense and pull in your stomach muscles to help keep your upper body still and provide a solid platform for your legs to push against.

other useful techniques efficient pedaling pp.40–41   drinking on the move pp.88–89

WEEK SIX: SESSION THREE

GROUP REPEATS

Cycling with others can make a ride more interesting; it also increases the training effect if you ride in single file, or in a "pace-line." The leading rider works the hardest because she must overcome more air resistance than those behind. Here, you take turns leading the group.

SESSION INFORMATION		
length	beg	30 mins
	int	45 mins
	adv	1hr
type	interval training	
terrain	flat or undulating	
intensity	▼ ●●○	⚡ ●●○ 🏊 ●●○

Ideally, you need three riders for this session. If you perform group repeats on the roads, be sure to choose ones that are less busy.

Begin by cycling for the time specified, building up to 75% MHR, then form a single-file line with one rider behind the other. The leader rides at more than 75% MHR, and cycles at a pace that the others can follow, however he or she should not exceed 85% MHR. After 1 minute, the front rider eases off and the

two followers overtake. Use the technique opposite to ensure that you overtake safely. Swap the lead for the number of times specified, and finish the session by riding at 60–70% MHR for 5 minutes.

If you do not know two people with the same fitness level as you, or you feel uncomfortable riding in a group, this session's fitness objectives can be achieved by riding on your own at 75% MHR for 1 minute, followed by riding at 60% MHR for 2 minutes.

TECHNIQUE: OVERTAKING

Riding in single file requires concentration. When following, stay close to the rider in front, but only as close as you feel comfortable. Do not follow directly behind the wheel of the cyclist in front, stay behind but just to one side, then if the rider slows suddenly, you will not run into them.

SESSION SUMMARY	Beginner	Intermediate	Advanced
▪ Cycle warm-up: Build up slowly to 75% MHR	10 mins	10 mins	10 mins
▪ Take turns to lead the group, riding at more than 75% MHR	1 mins	1 mins	1 mins
▪ Ride following group leader	2 mins	2 mins	2 mins
▪ Repeat lead/follow	× 5	× 10	× 15
▪ Complete session by riding at 60–70% MHR	5 mins	5 mins	5 mins
▪ Upper body: Lateral raise (p.56)	10 reps	15 reps	20 reps
▪ Core Exercises (pp.54–55)	10 reps	15 reps	20 reps
▪ Cool down by stretching (pp.52–53)			

1 Three cyclists ride in a line, with A in the lead and B and C following. Rider A flicks her outside elbow to indicate that she is ready to be overtaken.

2 Having indicated, rider A then slows down. Riders B and C check that the road is clear behind and then pull out. They continue to maintain a safe distance between them as they begin to overtake.

3 Riders B and C overtake rider A. They maintain a steady pace throughout the manoeuvre.

4 Rider B now leads the line with rider A at the rear. Riders C and A now follow, keeping a comfortable distance between them.

other useful techniques drinking on the move *pp.88–89* keeping a safe distance *p.93*

WEEK SIX: SESSION FOUR

UTILIZATION RIDE

This is a taxing day, but all your work so far has prepared you for it. Riding for a long period at utilization level requires focus—stay within the heart rate range specified, and use the technique opposite to negotiate any off-road obstacles that may slow you down.

<table>
<tr><th colspan="2">SESSION INFORMATION</th></tr>
<tr><td>length</td><td>beg 50 mins
int 1hr 10 mins
adv 1hr 30 mins</td></tr>
<tr><td>type</td><td>constant pace</td></tr>
<tr><td>terrain</td><td>undulating</td></tr>
<tr><td>intensity</td><td>●●● ●●● ●●○</td></tr>
</table>

Pedal hard
Push yourself, but stay within the specified heart rate range to get the full benefit of this session.

Start the session by building up slowly to 75% MHR for the time specified. Then, on an undulating course, increase the effort slightly and ride the main part of the session at 75–80% MHR. On hills, shift gear to stay within this heart rate range. If you go over 80% MHR on a climb, freewheel on the descent to allow your heart rate to drop. Finish the session by riding at 60–70% MHR for the time specified. This is a long and rigorous session, and you will use a lot of energy completing it. Remember to eat and drink regularly, but try not to stop riding in order to do so (*see pp.88–89*).

INDOOR SESSION ADAPTER
Build up to 70–75% MHR as specified. Then use the resistance of the spin bike or shift gears so that your heart rate fluctuates between 75–80% MHR. Beginners ride for 20 mins, Intermediate for 30 mins and Advanced for 40 mins. All levels complete session by riding at 60–70% MHR for 10 mins.

SESSION SUMMARY	Beginner	Intermediate	Advanced
■ Cycle warm-up: Build up slowly to 75% MHR	10 mins	10 mins	10 mins
■ Ride an undulating course at 75–80% MHR: Recover on descents	30 mins	45 mins	60 mins
■ Complete session by riding at 60–70% MHR	10 mins	15 mins	20 mins
■ Core Exercises (*pp.54–55*)	10 reps	15 reps	20 reps
■ Cool down by stretching (*pp.52–53*)			

TECHNIQUE: NEGOTIATING OBSTACLES

Here, the key is to shift your weight to help your balance and your traction, just as when negotiating uneven terrain or drop-offs. Only use this technique for tackling small obstacles such as fallen branches and logs. Remember, never ride over any obstacle unless you can see what is directly on the other side.

2 When the front wheel lands on the other side of the obstacle, move your body forward to unload the back wheel so that it can ride over.

1 As you approach the obstacle, slow down, get out of the saddle, and crouch down a little over the handlebars. Just before the obstacle, pull sharply upward on the handlebars and move your body back to lift the front wheel over it.

other useful techniques negotiating a drop-off *p.101* negotiating uneven terrain *pp.106–107*

WEEK SEVEN OVERVIEW

In this final week of the Program, I've combined training techniques and cycling skills from earlier sessions to create new and invigorating workouts. As usual, the sessions provide good aerobic workouts as well as strengthening, toning, and shaping your muscles. This is a tough week, but a varied one. Push yourself hard to meet the fitness challenges, and enjoy practicing the different skills you've learned.

Completing the program

The key to maintaining a good fitness level is to continuously challenge your body in different ways. Your body settles comfortably into routine. If you always cycle the same route at the same pace, you'll benefit less and less from your rides. The fantastic thing about cycling is that it can offer so much variety. Cycling on different terrains, varying your speed, changing gears, taking corners, and tackling hills all challenge your body in different ways.

In "Ascending Repeats" and "Putting It All Together," quick bursts of speed recruit fast-twitch muscles, then longer periods of effort provide an aerobic workout. In "Race Yourself," the focus is on building and maintaining speed.

In the final session, "Explore the Possibilities," you take the initiative. Design your own ride based on the sessions that you've enjoyed the most. The Program was designed to develop and improve your fitness level and then provide you with the tools, or techniques, to train your own way. Think about the next stage of using cycling as a way to build and maintain your fitness.

If you followed the Program at Beginner or Intermediate level, you might want to repeat it at a higher one. Or consider working toward a new challenge (*see pp.132–143*).

Cycling beyond the program
Continue to challenge yourself in the future, cycle regularly, and enjoy your improved fitness.

WEEK SEVEN AT A GLANCE

Mon ■ Active recovery. Light physical activity.

Tues Session1: Ascending Repeats
- ■ Interval training.
- ■ Initial stamina-booster work, then hard work/ recovery repeats that get progressively longer.
- ■ Shorter bursts of hard work tone and shape muscles, while longer repeats benefit the heart and lungs.

Weds ■ Active recovery, as on Monday.

Thurs Session 2: Putting It All Together
- ■ Constant pace.
- ■ A varied ride that incorporates techniques such as taking corners and riding hills.
- ■ Includes work at stamina-booster, utilization, and threshold levels.
- ■ A good aerobic and whole-body resistance workout.

Fri ■ Active recovery, as on Monday.

Sat Session 3: Race Yourself
- ■ Interval training.
- ■ Primarily a light aerobic workout, but with one intense sprinting effort which adds a resistance element to the session.
- ■ Some riding at active-recovery level.

Sun Session 4: Explore the Possibilities
- ■ Constant pace.
- ■ A final session to set you on your way: You decide where you go and what you do.

WEEK SEVEN: SESSION ONE

ASCENDING REPEATS

Here you repeat two types of sprints. The first intense sprint stimulates the fast-twitch muscles, then a series of progressively longer sprints build aerobic fitness. It is crucial that you push hard in the first sprint in order to benefit fully from the session.

Build up to and then ride for the time specified at 75% MHR. All fitness levels then cycle hard for 30 seconds and then recover. Then ride hard for 1 minute, not exceeding 85% MHR, then recover for 1 minute. Ride hard again for 2 minutes, but this time in the threshold range (80–85% MHR), followed by 2 minutes of riding easy. Beginners end the session here by riding at 60–70% MHR. Intermediate and advanced continue cycling hard then easy for the times specified, then finish by riding at 60–70% MHR.

SESSION INFORMATION

length	beg	30 mins
	int	45 mins
	adv	1hr 1 min
type		interval training
terrain		flat or undulating
intensity	● ● ●	● ● ●	● ● ●

TECHNIQUE: HARD SPRINTING

When sprinting for extended periods, start out of the saddle to put as much power as possible behind your pedaling. Then sit in the saddle, but sustain the effort by continuing to pedal hard.

SESSION SUMMARY	Beginner	Intermediate	Advanced
■ Cycle warm-up: Build up to then maintain 75% MHR	10 mins	15 mins	20 mins
■ Ride as hard as you can	30 secs	30 secs	30 secs
■ Ride easy to recover	30 secs	30 secs	30 secs
■ Ride hard, but do not exceed 85% MHR	1 min	1 min	1 min
■ Ride easy to recover	1 min	1 min	1 min
■ Ride at threshold level (80–85% MHR)	2 mins	2 mins	2 mins
■ Ride easy to recover	2 mins	2 mins	2 mins
■ Repeat threshold/easy		3/3 mins	3/3 mins
■ Repeat threshold/easy			4/4 mins
■ Complete session by riding at 60–70% MHR	13 mins	17 mins	20 mins
■ Core Exercises (pp.54–55)	10 reps	15 reps	20 reps
■ Cool down by stretching (pp.52–53)			

1 Start sprinting out of the saddle. Push down hard with one leg while pulling up with the other. Repeat this to build up speed, all the time pulling upward and back a bit on your handlebars with both arms.

2 Once you have built up speed, settle back in
the saddle with control—don't just drop into it.
Continue to pedal hard, pull on the handlebars, and use
your shoulders to help you power the pedals around.
Pull the handlebars with alternate arms to help each leg
as you pedal, rather than pulling upward equally.

other useful techniques sprint position *p.91* sprint-pedaling uphill *p.99*

WEEK SEVEN: SESSION TWO

PUTTING IT ALL TOGETHER

Aim to incorporate skills and techniques that you have learned earlier in the Program in today's ride. Try to find a circuit that takes you about 5 minutes to ride around when cycling hard. Ideally, it should also have two or three 90° corners and a hill.

SESSION INFORMATION		
length	beg	30 mins
	int	45 mins
	adv	1hr
type	constant pace	
terrain	undulating	
intensity		

TECHNIQUE: CORNERING

The best and quickest way to get round any corner is to take the straightest line through it: Start wide, cut in for the apex, then come out of it wide. Off-road, be aware of trail conditions: Avoid crossing loose surfaces, and, where they exist, use berms to help you get round. On-road, corner slowly and carefully in traffic (*see pp.36–37*).

lean into the turn
point your inside knee into the turn, keep your inside pedal up, and shift your weight over your outside leg

line up
slow down if you need to, and assess the corner; decide on the best line of attack; aim for the apex of the corner

THE SESSION

Once you have warmed up, ride hard on your circuit, doing laps, for the time specified. Do not exceed 85% MHR, but try to better your time on each lap. Concentrate on safe cornering and accelerating strongly out of corners *(see below)*. Try to set a good pace on climbs. Finish by riding at 60–70% MHR.

SESSION SUMMARY	Beginner	Intermediate	Advanced
■ Cycle warm-up: Build up to then maintain 75% MHR	10 mins	15 mins	20 mins
■ Ride quite hard on a circuit	10 mins	15 mins	20 mins
■ Complete session by riding at 60–70% MHR	10 mins	15 mins	20 mins
■ Core Exercises *(pp.54–55)*	10 reps	15 reps	20 reps
■ Cool down by stretching *(pp.52–53)*			

accelerate out
come out of the corner, and as the bike straightens up, pedal hard to power yourself forward and build up speed again

WEEK SEVEN: SESSION THREE

RACE YOURSELF

There is nothing better than competition for motivating a person to try harder. In today's session you ride a flat stretch of road or trail, set a good time, and then go back and try to beat it. Even if you don't better your time, you've won because your opponent is you.

SESSION INFORMATION

length	beg	38 mins
	int	43 mins
	adv	46 mins
type	interval training	
terrain	flat	
intensity	♥ ●●●	🏃 ●●● ✈ ●●○

Begin by riding for the time specified at 75% MHR. Choose a flat stretch of fairly straight road or trail, and note the direction of the wind. Ride hard, with the wind behind you, but do not exceed 80% MHR. Record your time for 1 mile. Then ride for 10 minutes at 60–70% MHR, and return to what was your finish line. Ride the same 1-mile stretch again, but this time cycle into the wind. Record your time. Finish by riding at 60–70% MHR.

SESSION SUMMARY	Beginner	Intermediate	Advanced
■ Cycle warm-up: Build up to then maintain 75% MHR	10 mins	15 mins	20 mins
■ Ride hard with wind behind; do not exceed 80% MHR.	1 mile (1.6km)	1 mile (1.6km)	1 mile (1.6km)
■ Ride at 60–70% MHR	10 mins	10 mins	10 mins
■ Ride hard into wind in opposite direction	1 mile (1.6km)	1 mile (1.6km)	1 mile (1.6km)
■ Complete session by riding at 60–70% MHR	10 mins	10 mins	10 mins
■ Upper body: Shoulder press (p.57)	10 reps	15 reps	20 reps
■ Core Exercises (pp.54–55)	10 reps	15 reps	20 reps
■ Cool down by stretching (pp.52–53)			

Making a U-turn
Check behind before you slow down, and check again before you turn; point your inside knee into the turn and keep the inner pedal up.

TIP

During the 10 mins of easy riding between the two efforts, pedal quite quickly in a low gear, but keep within the heart rate range. Halfway through this recovery period, stop, dismount and perform the hamstring stretch (see p.52). These two tips help you to stay loose and get really low and aerodynamic for the second effort.

TECHNIQUE: RIDING IN THE WIND

Learn how to take advantage of having the wind behind you, and use it to help increase your speed. Similarly, see how to make yourself aerodynamic so that you can ride as quickly as possible into the wind.

1 To take advantage of a following wind, hold the tops of the handlebars and keep your arms quite straight. Sit upright in the saddle, and allow your body to be blown along like a sail.

2 To ride quickly into the wind, you need to present as small a frontal area to it as possible. Lower your upper body so that your chest is parallel to the ground. Tuck in your elbows and keep your knees in as you pedal.

other useful techniques sprint position *p.91* cornering *pp.126–127*

WEEK SEVEN: SESSION FOUR

EXPLORE THE POSSIBILITIES

Today's session is self-explanatory. Cycle anywhere you like, and enjoy it. Reflect on what you have achieved and on possible future fitness goals. If you have completed the Program as a Beginner or Intermediate, consider following it again at a higher level.

<table>
<tr><td colspan="2">SESSION INFORMATION</td></tr>
<tr><td>length</td><td>beg I hr 20 mins
int I hr 45 mins
adv 2hrs</td></tr>
<tr><td>type</td><td>constant pace</td></tr>
<tr><td>terrain</td><td>any</td></tr>
<tr><td>intensity</td><td>♥ ●●●   ⚹ ●●●   ⛷ ●●○</td></tr>
</table>

Ride wherever you please at a pace you feel is comfortable, either on your own or with friends. If you feel happy doing so, make some harder efforts, but do not exceed 80% MHR. Try to ride further or for longer than you have done so far in the Program, but above all, enjoy yourself.

The day after this ride, have an easy day during which you rest. Then do the Rejuvenation Ride (*see pp.96–97*) and try the test again (*see pp.62–63*). After another easy day, do the Fitness Test on pages 58–59 and assess your progress. If you've worked hard, your fitness level will have improved. Consider embarking on the Program again, or set a new fitness challenge for yourself.

SESSION SUMMARY	Beginner	Intermediate	Advanced
■ Cycle warm-up: Slowly build up to 70% MHR	10 mins	10 mins	10 mins
■ Ride at comfortable pace not exceeding 80% MHR	1 hour 10 mins	1 hour 35 mins	1 hour 50 mins
■ Core Exercises (*pp.54–55*)	10 reps	15 reps	20 reps
■ Cool down by stretching (*pp.52–53*)			

INDOOR SESSION ADAPTER

Choose your favorite session from the Program and repeat it, but adapt it slightly. Cycle for longer, or make it more challenging by following it at a higher level.

Outward bound
Go out and enjoy your bike—you are a lot fitter than you were seven weeks ago.

other useful techniques climbing a hill economically *p.83* relaxed riding *pp.96–97*

Free-wheeling
You've achieved your goals and the open
road is yours: Keep fit, have fun and explore.

CHALLENGES

You've worked hard to complete the Program, now how can you build on what you've achieved so far? With your improved fitness level and armory of different cycling skills, a whole world of possibilities opens up to you. You might consider going on a cycling trip in a different country, or getting involved in a mass-participaton event in support of a charity, or even entering a race. The most important thing is to continue to set yourself challenges and to keep exploring new ways to enjoy yourself on your bike. Here I present five training programs that prepare you for a range of different challenges and which I hope will keep you cycling well into the future.

CYCLING VACATION

This six-week training program will prepare you for the physical challenges of a cycling vacation. It can be followed by anyone who has completed the seven-week Program and is suitable for all levels. Follow it at the same level as you did the seven-week Program. Whether you are cycling in familiar territory or discovering somewhere entirely new, traveling on a bike is a fantastic experience. You interact with your surroundings much more closely than you would when traveling by car, and you cover more ground than you would on foot. Added to that, you are boosting your fitness level by completing several days of stamina-boosting workouts.

Choosing a cycling trip

There are two options for touring holidays on the road, and both have their advantages. If you travel independently, you have the freedom to go wherever you please; you can plan your own route and tailor your trip to suit your interests. You may want to camp overnight, which will mean that you carry a tent, cooking equipment, and a change of clothes, or you can stay in hotels, which reduces your load.

The other option is to go with an organized tour. In this case a travel company will book overnight stops and carry all of your luggage for you. Generally, organized tours tend to be less arduous because they have to cater to different ability levels, but they often have very experienced guides, which can make a big difference in a foreign country. If you have never been on a cycling vacation, or if you have completed the Program at Beginner or Intermediate level, consider an organized tour—it is the best option for a first trip.

Training for your trip

You need plenty of stamina to ride for extended periods, and you need to be fit enough to ride for several days in succession. The main goal of this training regime is to work on your base level of aerobic fitness and boost your stamina so that you are strong enough to cycle for long periods every day. Some of the sessions include an element of resistance training, which will build muscular strength so that you can tackle any hills you might encounter with relative ease. In this program, I have scheduled two and eventually three days of consecutive training to help get you accustomed to the feeling of riding every day, as you will do on your trip.

Week	Monday	Tuesday
1	Active recovery: 20–30 mins of easy exercise	Stamina Booster (pp.66–67), but increase duration of 70–75% MHR part by 50% and decrease final 60–70% MHR by 50%
2	Active recovery: 20–30 mins of easy exercise	Basic Hills (pp.76–77), but increase duration of 75–80% MHR by 50%; reduce other parts to 10 mins each
3	Active recovery: 20–30 mins of easy exercise	Extended Utilization (pp.88–89), but increase duration of 75–80% MHR part by 25%
4	Active recovery: 20–30 mins of easy exercise	Ins and Outs (pp.106–107)
5	Active recovery: 20–30 mins of easy exercise	Stamina Booster (pp.66–67), but do session as Tuesday of week 1
6	Active recovery: 20–30 mins of easy exercise	Stamina Booster (pp.66–67)

Wednesday	Thursday	Friday	Saturday	Sunday
Active recovery: 20–30 minutes of easy exercise	Quick Spin (*pp. 68–69*), but increase duration of 60–75% MHR part by 50%	Active recovery: 20–30 mins of easy exercise	Relaxed Spin (*pp.80–81*), but increase duration of entire session by 25%	Long Leisurely Ride (*pp.72–73*), but increase duration of entire session by 25%
Active recovery: 20–30 mins of easy exercise	Basic Hills (*pp.76–77*), but increase duration of 75–80% MHR by 25%; reduce other parts to 10 mins	Active recovery: 20–30 mins of easy exercise	Power Pushes (*pp.70–71*), but increase duration of push to 20 seconds	Long Ride (*pp.82–83*), but increase duration of 70–75% part by 50%
Relaxed Spin (*pp.80–81*), but do session as Saturday of week 1	Active recovery: 20–30 mins of easy exercise	Active recovery: 20–30 mins of easy exercise	Sprints (*pp.90–91*)	Long Ride (*pp.82–83*), but try to ride further than you have done so far
Extended Utilization (*pp.88–89*), but do session as Tuesday of week 3	Active recovery: 20–30 mins of easy exercise	Stamina Booster (*pp.66–67*), but do session as Tuesday of week 1	Relaxed Spin (*pp.80–81*), but do session as Saturday of week 1	Utilization Ride (*pp.110–111*)
Basic Hills (*pp.76–77*), but do session as Thursday of week 2	Active recovery: 20–30 mins of easy exercise	Active recovery: 20–30 mins of easy exercise	Stamina Booster (*pp.66–67*), but do session as Tuesday of week 1	Long Ride (*pp.82–83*), but do session as Sunday of week 2
Active recovery: 20–30 mins of easy exercise	Sprints (*pp.90–91*)	Active recovery: 20–30 mins of easy exercise	Long Ride (*pp.82–83*): but decrease duration of session by 25%	Relaxed Spin (*pp.80–81*)

OFF-ROAD CYCLING TRIP

Cycling off-road is generally more challenging than its on-road equivalent because it requires good off-road bike skills and more physical strength to cope with the varied terrains. Off-road touring can be exciting though—it tests cycling skills, but it also requires strategic planning, since you have to weigh up the energy costs of crossing different terrains to reach your objective. This challenge is suitable for anyone who has completed the seven-week Program, and should be followed at the same level.

Choosing an off-road touring trip

The level at which you followed the Program has a bearing on the kind of off-road cycling trip you should choose. If you completed the Program at the Beginner or Intermediate level, for your first off-road trip it is probably best to sign up for an organized tour. There are off-road tours for every ability level, so be sure to ask the company how demanding the rides will be. You could also undertake a center-based tour, where you find accommodation in an area that interests you and then take day trips from your base, picking routes that match your off-road cycling experience. More advanced cyclists could consider traveling entirely independently: You can plan your own route, carry equipment, and camp overnight.

Training for your trip

Whatever holiday you pick, you will need to build up your stamina and get used to riding for several consecutive days. This six-week program will build your base level of fitness so that you can ride for long periods, and will also develop extra muscle power so that you can tackle hills effectively. On top of this, several of these sessions will help to hone your off-road cycling skills.

Try to do as many of the sessions as you can in the program off road. If you plan to carry equipment with you when traveling, even if it's just a backpack with food and spares for a day trip, do at least two of the sessions in weeks three and four with that equipment. It is a good idea to get used to the feeling of carrying extra weight—it makes a ride more challenging but it also changes the way your bike handles.

Week	Monday	Tuesday
1	Active recovery: 20–30 mins of easy exercise	Stamina Booster (pp.66–67), but increase duration of 70–75% MHR part by 50%; increase final 60–70% MHR part by 50%
2	Active recovery: 20–30 mins of easy exercise	Corner Pushes (pp.78–79), but add 5–10 mins of riding at 60–75% MHR to end of session
3	Active recovery: 20–30 mins of easy exercise	Stamina Booster (pp.66–67) as Tuesday of week 1, but increase duration of 70–75% MHR part by a further 25%
4	Active recovery: 20–30 mins of easy exercise	Deep Muscle Repeats (pp.116–117)
5	Active recovery: 20–30 mins of easy exercise	Stamina Booster (pp.66–67), but do session as Tuesday of week 3
6	Active recovery: 20–30 mins of easy exercise	Putting it All Together (pp.126–127), but reduce hard riding part by 25%

Wednesday	Thursday	Friday	Saturday	Sunday
Active recovery: 20–30 mins of easy exercise	Stamina Booster (pp.66–67) as Tuesday, but increase duration of 70–75% MHR part by a further 25%	Active recovery: 20–30 mins of easy exercise	Power Pushes (pp.70–71)	Adventure Ride (pp.100–101); seek out especially challenging terrain to practice skills
Active recovery: 20–30 mins of easy exercise	Basic Hills (pp.76–77), but increase 75–80% MHR part by 25%; all levels do 10 mins 60–70% MHR	Active recovery: 20–30 mins of easy exercise	Power Pushes (pp.70–71)	Group Ride (pp.92–93), but ride further than you have done in the Program so far
Hard Easy (pp.86–87)	Active recovery: 20–30 mins of easy exercise	Active recovery: 20–30 mins of easy exercise	Hill Sprints (pp.98–99)	Adventure Ride (pp.100–101); make this your longest ride; carry food and spares in a backpack
Hill Threshold Repeats (pp.114–115)	Active recovery: 20–30 mins of easy exercise	Ins and Outs (pp.106–107)	Sprints (pp.90–91)	Utilization Ride (pp.110–111)
Basic Hills (pp.76–77), but do session as Thursday of week 2	Active recovery: 20–30 mins of easy exercise	Active recovery: 20–30 mins of easy exercise	Stamina Booster (pp.66–67), but do session as Tuesday of week 1	Adventure Ride (pp.100–101); but do session as Sunday of week 1
Active recovery: 20–30 mins of easy exercise	Hill Sprints (pp.98–99), but Beginners do 1 repeat, Intermediate 2, Advanced 3	Active recovery: 20–30 mins of easy exercise	Adventure Ride (pp.100–101)	Relaxed Spin (pp.80–81)

LONG-DISTANCE RIDE

This five-week program will prepare you for riding a long distance such as 40–50 miles (65–80km), which you might do if you are taking part in a charity ride or mass-participation event. Riding a long distance as part of an organized event provides company, encouragement, and often food and drinks to keep you going along the way, too. In this program you also practice skills to help you get accustomed to riding in a group. This program is suitable for all levels. If you followed the seven-week Program at Beginner or Intermediate level, this training regime will prepare you for a 40–50 mile (65–80km) ride, but if you followed it at Advanced level, you could use it to train for a longer distance such as 100 miles (160km). Follow this program at the same level as you did the seven-week one.

Finding a charity ride

Contact local bike shops, cycling clubs, and sports centers, or search the internet for information on charity rides taking place locally and nationally. High-profile charity rides are organized all over the world. One option is Ride for the Roses, which raises money for the Lance Armstrong Cancer Foundation each year.

Training for a long-distance ride

Not surprisingly, the focus of this program is stamina. To prepare your body for maintaining constant speed over a long distance, you need to improve its efficiency by training at the stamina-booster level (70–75% MHR). You also need to accustom your body to long hours in the saddle. You will finish the ride very stiff and sore if you don't do at least one practice long-distance run before your challenge. As a result, the longer Sunday rides in this program are the most important sessions. However I've also included some training at higher heart rates to help you cope with any extra efforts on the ride, such as riding up hills or into a headwind.

If you are participating in a charity ride, you will be riding as part of a large group. During the Group Ride (week 2, Sunday), practice following behind other riders and swapping the lead (see Overtaking, pp.118–119). In headwinds, a cyclist following close behind another uses at least one third less energy. This can be a big help on a long ride.

Week	Monday	Tuesday
1	Active recovery: 20–30 mins of easy exercise	Stamina Booster (pp.66–67), but increase duration of 70–75% MHR and decrease duration of final 60–70% MHR by 50%
2	Active recovery: 20–30 mins of easy exercise	Basic Hills (pp.76–77), but increase duration of 75–80% MHR part by 50%; reduce other parts to 10 mins each
3	Active recovery: 20–30 mins of easy exercise	Extended Utilization (pp.88–89), but increase duration of 75–80% MHR part by 25%
4	Active recovery: 20–30 mins of easy exercise	Hill Threshold Repeats (pp.114–115)
5	Active recovery: 20–30 mins of easy exercise	Flat Threshold Repeats (pp.104–105), but do only 1 repeat at 80–85% MHR

Wednesday	Thursday	Friday	Saturday	Sunday
Active recovery: 20–30 mins of easy exercise	Basic Hills (pp.76–77)	Active recovery: 20–30 mins of easy exercise	Power Pushes (pp.70–71)	Long Ride (pp.82–83), but ride at least 10% longer than you did in the Program
Active recovery: 20–30 mins of easy exercise	Corner Pushes (pp.78–79)	Active recovery: 20–30 mins of easy exercise	Sprints (pp.90–91)	Group ride (pp.92–93) but ride at least 10% longer than you did in the Program
Active recovery: 20–30 mins of easy exercise	Hard and Easy (pp.86–87)	Active recovery: 20–30 mins of easy exercise	Hill Sprints (pp.98–99)	Long Ride (pp.82–83), but ride 75% of the distance of your planned ride
Active recovery: 20–30 mins of easy exercise	Extended Utilization (pp.88–89), but increase duration of 75–80% MHR part by 50%	Active recovery: 20–30 mins of easy exercise	Sprints (pp.90–91)	Long Ride (pp.82–83), but ride same duration as Sunday week 1
Active recovery: 20–30 mins of easy exercise	Ins and Outs (pp.106–107), but reduce the number of accelerations to 80% MHR by 50%	Active recovery: 20–30 mins of easy exercise	Sprints (pp.90–91)	Long-distance ride

TIME TRIAL

Time trials are organized by cycling clubs all over the world, and are a great introduction to road cycling competition. In a time trial, competitors start individually at one-minute intervals and race against the clock. The winner is the cyclist who completes the course in the fastest time. A time trial can be organized over any distance, but this program prepares you for a 10 mile (16km) race. This challenge is suitable for all levels, and should be followed at the same level as you completed the seven-week Program. If you don't feel confident about competing in a race, you could complete this program, ride your own course, and compare your time to official race times for a circuit of the same length (race times are available on the internet).

Whether you compete in an official time trial race or set your own course and do a time trial on your own, cycling hard (at threshold level, or 80–85% MHR) for 10 miles (16km) is an impressive achievement in itself.

Choosing a time trial

Approach your local cycling club, bike shop, or sports center for information on time trials in your area. The internet is also a good place to search for contacts.

If you aren't ready to compete in an official time trial, consider arranging one on your own. Choose familiar roads, and measure a 10 mile (16km) course either on your bike with a cycle computer, or drive the course in a car and measure it on the odometer. Circuits make the best courses, but make sure that all corners are on the same side of the road as you ride.

Training for a time trial

The main thrust of this program is threshold training in order to prepare your body for riding at high intensity. However I have also included some longer sessions that will help maintain your base level of fitness and boost stamina.

Another factor that will determine the speed you achieve over 10 miles (16km) is the amount of power you can deliver to the pedals. The more power you apply, the faster you'll go when working at threshold level. Sessions such as "Ascending Repeats," "Standing Starts," and "Sprints" will help to build power and speed and improve this aspect of your riding. Adjust this program accordingly if your race is not on a Sunday.

Week	Monday	Tuesday
1	Active recovery: 20–30 mins of easy exercise	Hard and Easy (pp.86–87), but do 2 hard/easy repeats with 5 mins at 60–70% MHR between them
2	Active recovery: 20–30 mins of easy exercise	Flat Threshold Repeats (pp.104–105), but reduce 60–70% MHR riding time between repeats by 50%
3	Active recovery: 20–30 mins of easy exercise	Flat Threshold Repeats (pp.104–105), but do session as Tuesday week 2, and do one extra repeat
4	Active recovery: 20–30 mins of easy exercise	Ascending Repeats (pp.124–125)
5	Active recovery: 20–30 mins of easy exercise	Ascending Repeats (pp.124–125), but only do session up to and including 2 mins at 80–85% MHR

Wednesday	Thursday	Friday	Saturday	Sunday
Active recovery: 20–30 mins of easy exercise	Corner Pushes (*pp.78–79*)	Active recovery: 20–30 mins of easy exercise	Power Pushes (*pp.70–71*)	Utilization Repeats (*pp.110–111*), but cut the riding time at 60–70% MHR between each repeat to 3 mins
Active recovery: 20–30 mins of easy exercise	Ins and Outs (*pp.106–107*) but do 2 extra pace increases to 80% MHR	Active recovery: 20–30 mins of easy exercise	Hill Sprints (*pp.98–99*)	Long Ride (*pp.82–83*)
Active recovery: 20–30 mins of easy exercise	Flat Threshold Repeats (*pp.104–105*), but do session as Tuesday week 2	Active recovery: 20–30 mins of easy exercise	Sprints (*pp.90–91*)	Utilization Repeats (*pp.110–111*), but do session as Sunday week 1, and ride close to 80% MHR for each repeat
Active recovery: 20–30 mins of easy exercise	Ascending Repeats (*pp.124–125*)	Active recovery: 20–30 mins of easy exercise	Standing Starts (*pp.108–109*)	Long Ride (*pp.82–83*)
Active recovery: 20–30 mins of easy exercise	Hill Sprints (*pp.98–99*)	Active recovery: 20–30 mins of easy exercise	Standing Starts (*pp.108–109*)	Time trial

MOUNTAIN BIKE RACE

This is a more advanced challenge. Racing off-road requires stamina, speed, fitness, and skill. Although bikers of any ability can take part in a race, I recommend that Beginners go back and successfully complete the Program at Intermediate level before attempting a mountain bike race. Intermediate and Advanced level riders should follow this program at the same level as they did the seven-week one.

Finding a mountain bike race

Find out about races in your area by checking mountain bike magazines, looking on the internet, or contacting local bike shops, cycling clubs, or sports centers. Races are usually organized for different ability levels, from novice to elite, as well as by age group and gender.

Training for a mountain bike race

For a mountain bike race you need to be able to ride at fairly high intensity—threshold level—for a considerable length of time, maybe as long as an hour, even when competing as a novice. You also need power to accelerate from the start to get yourself into a good position for the narrow sections of the course. Added to that, on hilly courses you need to be able to climb well and descend safely. On any course you need to be technically proficient on your bike.

I've included several threshold sessions in this program, plus some work to keep your stamina up. Sessions such as "Standing Starts" and "Hill Sprints" will increase your power. Before you start training, review and practice the off-road skills and techniques outlined in this book. Start slowly, and build up speed as you gain confidence. Taking the correct line through a corner, or not having to dismount for a drop-off or log will be invaluable in the race.

A word of warning: Never take risks with obstacles, corners, or descents. Only ride over obstacles or drop-offs, or take descents, when you are confident you can manage them. It is quicker to carry your bike down a rocky descent than it is to ride down and crash. Your pride heals more quickly than your skin or bones.

Week	Monday	Tuesday
1	Active recovery: 20–30 mins of easy exercise	Flat Threshold Repeats (*pp.104–105*), but do an extra threshold/recovery repeat; reduce final 60–70% MHR by 50%
2	Active recovery: 20–30 mins of easy exercise	Hill Threshold Repeats (*pp.114–115*)
3	Active recovery: 20–30 mins of easy exercise	Hill Threshold Repeats (*pp.114–115*), but reduce recovery time between repeats by 50%
4	Active recovery: 20–30 mins of easy exercise	Putting It All Together (*pp.126–127*), but increase time riding hard by 50%; decrease final 60–70% MHR by 50%
5	Active recovery: 20–30 mins of easy exercise	Putting It All Together (*pp.126–127*), but decrease time riding hard by 50%

Wednesday	Thursday	Friday	Saturday	Sunday
Active recovery: 20–30 mins of easy exercise	Hard and Easy (*pp.86–87*)	Active recovery: 20–30 mins of easy exercise	Standing Starts (*pp.108–109*)	Adventure Ride (*pp.100–101*), but ride for at least 10% longer than you did in the Program
Active recovery: 20–30 mins of easy exercise	Deep Muscle Repeats (*pp.116–117*)	Active recovery: 20–30 mins of easy exercise	Hill Sprints (*pp.98–99*)	Utilization Ride (*pp.120–121*), but use challenging terrain for 75–80% MHR part of session
Active recovery: 20–30 mins of easy exercise	Putting It All Together (*pp.126–127*)	Active recovery: 20–30 mins of easy exercise	Standing Starts (*pp.108–109*)	Adventure Ride (*pp.100–101*) as Sunday week 1, but concentrate on skills and techniques
Active recovery: 20–30 mins of easy exercise	Hill Threshold Repeats (*pp.114–115*)	Active recovery: 20–30 mins of easy exercise	Hill Sprints (*pp.98–99*)	Utilization Ride (*pp.120–121*) as Sunday week 2, but ride closer to 80% MHR in main part of session
Active recovery: 20–30 mins of easy exercise	Hill Sprints (*pp.90–91*)	Active recovery: 20–30 mins of easy exercise	Sprints (*pp.110–111*)	Race

BIKE CARE
AND REPAIR

A well-maintained bike cries out to be ridden. In this section I show you how to clean your bike, check for potential problems, and repair a puncture (although I hope that you don't get many of those). Clean your bike regularly, not only because it will look better, but because it will run more smoothly and be far less likely to experience mechanical problems that can ruin an enjoyable ride. Carry out regular saftety checks too, as these will help to keep you aware of safety issues before they pose a danger to you. At the end of this section there is a troubleshooting chart to help diagnose and then remedy common problems. There is a helpful illustration of a bike too, to help you locate the different parts.

CLEANING YOUR BIKE

Bikes generally don't require a great deal of maintenance as most of their working parts are sealed, but some are open to the elements. The chain and gears in particular should be regularly cleaned and freshly lubricated to keep them in good working order. You will need some degreasing fluid (available from bike shops), a bucket of hot, soapy water, different-sized stiff-bristled brushes, and two sponges.

1 Remove both wheels from the bike and either put the frame in a stand or hang it up by its saddle. You will need a chainholder, a device that keeps tension in the chain when there is no rear wheel. Place this where the rear wheel was so that the chain can run freely.

2 Place a tray under the bike to catch any drips. Apply degreaser to the chain, chainsets, and front and rear derailleur (*see pp.154–155*) to remove any grit and old oil. Be sure to cover each link of the chain, then leave the degreaser to soak in for about 5 minutes.

3 Use a sponge to apply hot, soapy water to the parts you have degreased, and wash off all the old oil and dirt. Keep one sponge to use for just this job, since it will get very dirty. Wrap the sponge around the chain and turn a pedal to run the chain through the sponge so you can clean it thoroughly.

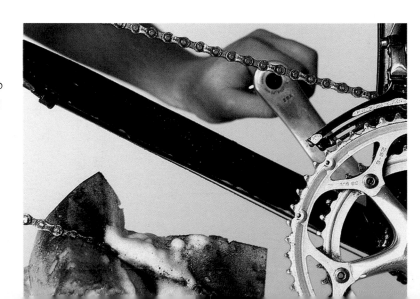

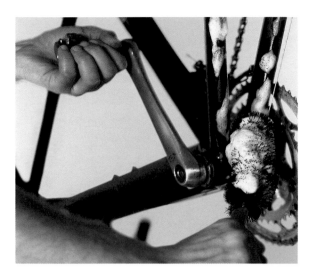

4 Use another sponge to apply plenty of soapy water to the rest of the bike. Work the soap in behind intricate parts such as the brakes, and use a stiff-bristled brush to clean under the bike where grime accumulates. Then rinse everything off with clean water, and dry the bike with a clean cloth.

5 Use a cassette scraper, or another similar thin tool, to scrape out any debris that has accummulated between the sprockets. Then apply degreaser and leave it to soak in for about 5 minutes. With a stiff-bristled brush and some hot soapy water, wash off the degreaser and any old lubricant and dirt.

6 Clean the brakes and small, difficult-to-access parts such as brake arms and pads with a soapy sponge. Use a stiff-bristled brush and soapy water to clean the cassette and between the sprockets. Then use the sponge to clean the underside of the saddle.

7 Use another clean brush (never a dirty one as you may transfer oil to your tires) and soapy water to wash the tires, rims, hubs, and spokes of your wheels. Then lightly lubricate the chain and the moving parts—the front and rear derailleurs.

ROUTINE SAFETY CHECKS

Before going out on a ride, get into the habit of performing these simple safety checks. They will only take a couple of minutes, and they will minimize the chances of a breakdown or accident due to equipment failure. The same checks apply for road, mountain, and hybrid bikes. If you do discover a problem, get it fixed straight away. Do it yourself, if you can, or take your bike to a bike repair shop.

FRAME CHECKS

It happens very rarely, but bike frames can suffer from metal or weld fatigue. In this case, do check your bike's warranty, as it may well be covered under it.

Perform regular checks before each ride and during the cleaning process to be sure that you catch any potential problems.

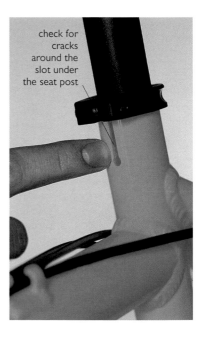

check for cracks around the slot under the seat post

1 Run a finger under the down tube where it joins the head tube. If you feel a ripple on the surface of the tube, it is fatigued. Visually check for cracks to the weld here, too. Get any chips or scratches to the frame's paintwork touched up to prevent possible corrosion.

2 Check around the area where the chainstay bridge is braised to the chain stays, and visually check the frame welds where the crank assembly fits into the frame. Check all frame welds regularly. Also check for cracks around bottle cage fittings and brake and gear cable guides.

3 Examine the slot under the saddle where the bolt attaches to the seat post, since cracks can sometimes form below this. If you ever replace the seat post, make sure it is the correct size for your frame. Fitting even a slightly smaller one can cause a crack.

PRE-RIDE SAFETY CHECKS

Carry out these four safety checks before every ride. In most cases you will find nothing wrong, but it is always better to be cautious. Regular checks provide useful information about how your bike is wearing.

the handlebars should not move independently of the front wheel

apply the front brake and push forward; any movement in the steering assembly means that the headset needs attention

1 Check the steering by holding the front wheel between your legs and trying to turn the handlebars. If they move independently of the front wheel, or if you can twist them upward, get the bike checked out.

2 Simultaneously apply the front and rear brakes fully, and push the bike forward. If you have to pull the brake levers back all the way or if either of the wheels rotates, your brakes need servicing.

3 Slowly spin the front wheel and then the rear wheel. Check each tire for cuts, splits, excessive wear, or bulges in the tread and sidewall. Any of these could cause a blow out. If you find a problem, replace the tire.

4 With the rear wheel lifted clear off the ground, run through the gears to check that they are properly adjusted. Stiff gears or a jumping chain can be dangerous because they distract you when cycling along.

REPAIRING A PUNCTURE

The best way to deal with a puncture when you are out on your bike is to replace the punctured inner tube, rather than try to repair it on the spot. Always carry a spare inner tube along with a set of tire levers and an inflator. Then you can repair the punctured tube later and use that as your spare. Always carry your puncture repair kit too, just in case you puncture a second time on a ride.

apply adhesive to an area just larger than your patch

2 Inflate the tube so that you can hear air escaping from the puncture. Mark the hole with the crayon from your repair kit. Let out any air, and spread a thin layer of adhesive over and around the hole.

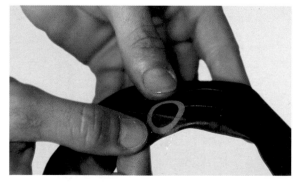

1 Remove the wheel from the bike, place one tire lever between the tire and the edge of the wheel rim, and lift part of the tire from the rim. Hook this first lever to a spoke, insert a second lever close to it, and push it forward, running it around the circumference of the rim to remove one side of the tire. Remove the tube.

3 Allow a few minutes for the adhesive to become tacky—it should change from clear to opaque. Peel the backing off the repair patch and press it firmly onto the adhesive, holding it for at least 1 minute. Check that the patch has formed a good seal and that all its edges are flat.

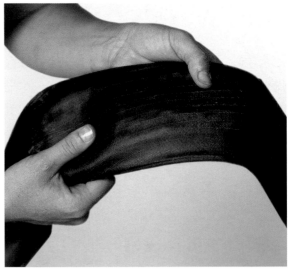

4 Dust some chalk over the patch to prevent any excess adhesive from sticking to the inside of the tire. Some repair kits contain powdered chalk, others have a stick of chalk that you have to scrape with sandpaper to make chalk.

5 Take the rest of the tire off the rim, check the outside, then turn it inside out and look and feel for anything sticking into it before fitting the tube. If you find something, remove it from the outside of the tire. Consider changing your tire after your ride.

6 Put one side of the tire back onto the rim. Then slightly inflate the tube, insert the valve into the rim valve hole, and work the tube under the tire so that it sits on the rim. Push the valve upward and, starting from the valve, lift the other side of the tire, section by section, over the edge of the rim. Pull the valve down and pinch the tire, section by section, to check that the tube isn't trapped between it and the rim. Then inflate the tire.

Checking the tire
Make sure the tire hasn't trapped the tube underneath it before you inflate the tube fully.

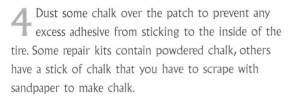

TIP
Another way to locate a puncture is to immerse the tube, section by section, in a bowl of water and look for bubbles.

TROUBLESHOOTING

When something goes wrong with your bike, even if you don't plan to fix it yourself, it helps to know the possible cause of the problem. This chart lists common problems along with possible causes and solutions. Consult Anatomy of a Bike (see *pp.154–155*) for help locating the different parts.

    The drivetrain of your bike relates to how your power from pedaling is transferred into forward motion; this section covers the pedals, chain and chainset, and gears. The steering and wheels includes anything to do with handlebars, forks, and wheels. The brake category is self-explanatory. Suspension refers to bikes that have suspension forks, or any other form of shock absorption.

    Reduce the likelihood of problems occurring by having your bike serviced at least twice a year—for example, at the start and end of winter. Consult one of the many books available on the subject, or visit a good bike shop—the staff are often experts in the field of bike repair.

    Sophisticated bikes, such as those made of high-tech materials like carbon fiber, or lightweight full-suspension mountain bikes, need regular expert attention. However, they are a joy to ride, so never let that put you off buying one.

Look after your bike
Service your bike regularly; deal with any problems that arise immediately, otherwise they may affect your safety.

	Problem
Drivetrain	The chain will not shift onto a smaller sprocket or chainring.
	The chain will not shift onto a larger sprocket or it shifts but does not run smoothly on it.
	The chain shifts cleanly, but jumps on the sprockets when pressure is applied to the
Steering and wheels	When you apply the front brake and push the bike forward, the headset moves forward relative to the head tube.
	A sudden snapping noise comes from a wheel while riding.
	When pedaling forward, the cassette spins but there is no drive to the bike.
Brakes	The brakes are hard to apply, and/or sluggish to release.
	You have to pull the brake lever a long way before the brakes engage.
	The brake pads contact the braking surface without pulling the brake levers too far but are ineffective at slowing the bike.
Suspension	The fork regularly reaches the limit of its travel (bottoms out).
	The front wheel judders up and down when cornering.

Cause	Solution
Grit has become lodged inside the cable housing, or the cable lubrication has dried up.	Get your shifters and cables serviced at a bike shop.
The cable has stretched or the relevant derailleur is poorly adjusted.	Shift to the smallest chainring or sprocket, loosen the cable clamp bolt on each derailleur, tighten the cable, re-tighten the bolt.
The chain has a stiff link; or the chain or sprockets, or both, are worn; or a chainring may be bent.	Get your chain examined for stiff links and/or wear.
The headset is loose or worn.	Get your headset serviced.
A spoke may have broken.	Have the spoke replaced and the wheel rim straightened or "trued."
The freehub body is worn.	Get the freehub body replaced.
Grit and dirt is inside the cable housing, or the lubrication on the inner cables has dried up.	Have your brakes serviced.
The pads are wearing down or the cable has slipped through the clamp bolt.	Have your brakes serviced.
There is grease on the pads, foreign objects are embedded in them, or they are wearing unevenly.	Have your brakes serviced.
With air/oil forks, not enough air is in the system. With coil/oil forks, too light a spring is fitted.	Either buy a shock pump (a tool for putting air into air/oil suspension systems), and pump more air into your forks, or get stiffer springs fitted to coil/oil forks.
The fork's rebound is set too fast.	Refer to the owner's manual, and use the relevant adjuster on the fork to reduce its rebound speed.

ANATOMY OF A BIKE

Use this annotated road bike to help familiarize you with the anatomy of your bike. Although features such as handlebars and brakes will differ between road, mountain, and hybrid bikes, the basic mechanism is the same: A chain drives the rear wheel and gears, and most brakes are connected by cables. On mountain bikes, you will find V-brakes, not callipers. V-brakes do not clog with mud and are ideal for off-road use. You might also find disc brakes on mountain bikes, which are either operated by cables or hydraulics. Some bikes have enclosed hub gear systems, not the derailleur type shown here, although these are quite rare. Refer to this illustration when consulting the Troubleshooting chart (see pp.152–153). Some useful basic terms are defined in the Glossary, opposite.

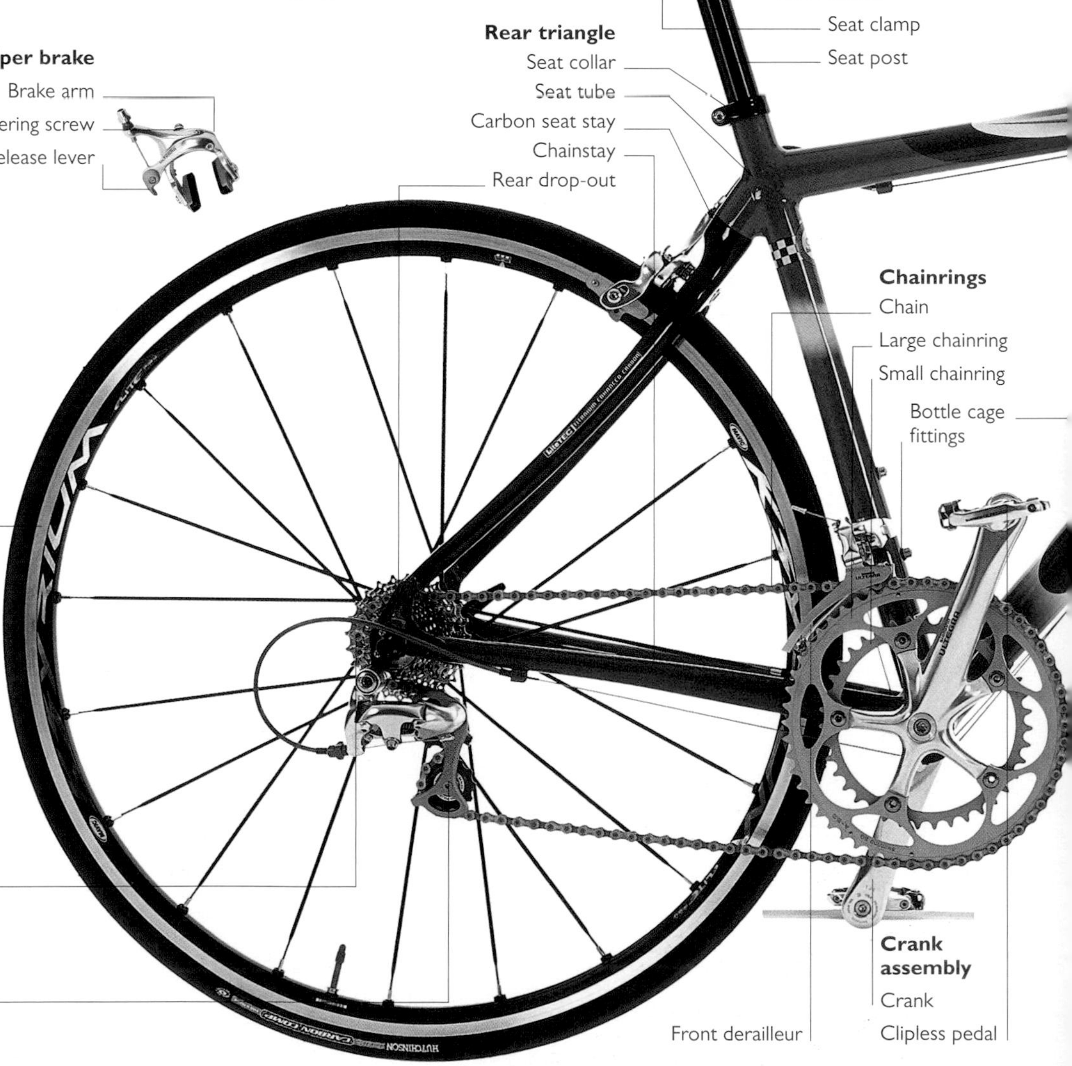

Rear caliper brake
Brake arm
Centering screw
Quick-release lever

Saddle and seat post
Saddle
Seat clamp
Seat post

Rear triangle
Seat collar
Seat tube
Carbon seat stay
Chainstay
Rear drop-out

Chainrings
Chain
Large chainring
Small chainring
Bottle cage fittings

Rear wheel

Sprockets (which fit on the freehub)

Rear derailleur

Front derailleur

Crank assembly
Crank
Clipless pedal

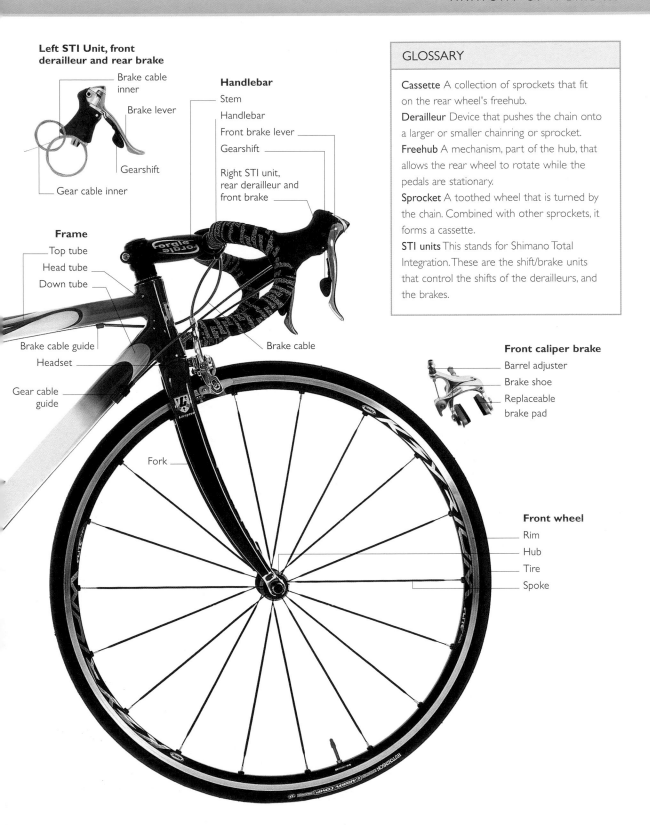

Left STI Unit, front derailleur and rear brake

Brake cable inner
Brake lever
Gearshift
Gear cable inner

Handlebar

Stem
Handlebar
Front brake lever
Gearshift
Right STI unit, rear derailleur and front brake

Frame

Top tube
Head tube
Down tube
Brake cable guide
Headset
Gear cable guide

Brake cable

Fork

GLOSSARY

Cassette A collection of sprockets that fit on the rear wheel's freehub.
Derailleur Device that pushes the chain onto a larger or smaller chainring or sprocket.
Freehub A mechanism, part of the hub, that allows the rear wheel to rotate while the pedals are stationary.
Sprocket A toothed wheel that is turned by the chain. Combined with other sprockets, it forms a cassette.
STI units This stands for Shimano Total Integration. These are the shift/brake units that control the shifts of the derailleurs, and the brakes.

Front caliper brake

Barrel adjuster
Brake shoe
Replaceable brake pad

Front wheel

Rim
Hub
Tire
Spoke

RESOURCES

ORGANIZATIONS

Adventure Cycling Association

150 East Pine Street
PO Box 8308
Missoula, MT 59802
USA
Tel: +1 800 755 2453
info@adventurecycling.org
www.adventurecycling.org
A bicycle-touring association that produces maps, tour itineraries, and a magazine for its 42,000 members.

America Bikes

1612 K Street NW
Suite 800
Washington, DC 20006
USA
Tel: +1 202 833 8080
info@americabikes.org
www.americabikes.org
This is a coalition of eight major cycling organizations working to help develop a seamless bicycle transportation network, ensure that new road projects are safe for cyclists and pedestrians, and support a Safe Route to School program.

Bicycle Federation of America

1506 21st Street NW
Suite 200
Washington, DC 200036
USA
Tel: +1 202 463 6622
info@bikewalk.org
www.bikewalk.org
This organization is involved in bicycle advocacy, public policy, planning, and facilities.

International Mountain Bicycling Association (IMBA)

1121 Broadway, Suite 203
PO Box 7578
Boulder, CO 80306
Tel: +1 303 545 9011
info@imba.com
www.imba.com
This body works to keep trails open for mountain bikes by encouraging responsible riding and supporting volunteer trail work. It produces an excellent trail-building manual.

The National Byway

PO Box 128
Newark
Notts NG23 6BL
UK
Tel: +44 (0) 1636 636818
www.thenationalbyway.org
This organization has mapped 4,000 miles of lightly used roads that are suitable for cyclists and which link together heritage sites.

Sustrans Information Service

PO Box 21
Bristol BS99 2HA
UK
Tel: +44 (0) 117 929 0888
www.sustrans.org.uk
This body has created the 6,000-mile British National Cycle Network of cyclist-only and lightly used roads. It is currently working with other bodies to create Eurovelo, a network of cycle-friendly routes across the whole continent.

WEBSITES FOR CYCLING ADVOCACY

www.crankmail.com
A directory of sites concerning cyclists and the law in the US.

www.bicycling.about.com
Information on bike advocacy, with links to other bike advocacy sites.

WEBSITES FOR CYCLING CLUBS

www.geocities.cp./colosseum/613
Website of bicycle clubs in the US.

MAGAZINES

Bicycling Magazine
1612 K Street NW
Suite 800
Washington, DC 20006
USA
Tel +1 202 882 1333
www.bikeleague.org
Supplied to members by the League of American Bicyclists, which fights for cyclists' rights in the US.

Mountain Bike
2509 Empire Avenue
Suite 2
Burbank, CA 91504
USA
www.mountainbike.com
Tests and reviews bikes and other equipment. Includes rides, tips, and event listings.

Cycling Weekly and
Mountain Bike Rider
IPC Media
5th Floor
Focus House
9 Dingwall Avenue
Croydon CR9 2TAA
UK
www.ipc.co.uk
Cycling Weekly
General cycling news as well as coverage of British and European road and track racing. It includes tests and reviews, riding tips, and event listings.

Mountain Bike Rider
Covers all aspects of mountain bike riding. Provides routes to ride in the UK and elsewhere. It includes tests and reviews of bikes and other products, riding tips, and event listings.

Cycling Plus, Mountain Biking UK and
What Mountain Bike?
Future Publishing
Beauford Court
30 Monmouth Street
Bath BA1 2BW
UK
Subscriptions +44 (0) 870 444 8470
Cycling Plus
Covers all aspects of road cycling. Tests and reviews bikes and other equipment. Includes cycling news, riding tips, and event listings.
Mountain Biking UK
Tests and reviews bikes and other equipment. Includes route suggestions, rides around the world, tips, and event listings.
What Mountain Bike?
A consumer's guide that tests and reviews bikes and equipment. Contains up-to-date listings of bike specifications; it also features riding tips.

INDEX

ACKNOWLEDGMENTS

AUTHOR'S ACKNOWLEDGMENTS

Nasim Mawji for her skilled, knowledgeable, and patient editing; Miranda Harvey for making the book come alive; Russell Sadur for his superb photography; and Nina Duncan for doing everything else on the photo shoot, and for being a brilliant traveling companion. I would also like to thank all of the models for their patience, in particular Heather Kahl and her family for not only modeling, but also for being such kind hosts. Special thanks to Trevor Kahl for lending us his weights.

PUBLISHER'S ACKNOWLEDGMENTS

Dorling Kindersley would like to thank photographer Russell Sadur and his assistant, Nina Duncan. Thanks to our tireless models (who also helped to source locations): Lecia Zulak, Heather Kahl, and Jonathon Farrell. Thanks also to Matt Tongue for sourcing bikes and equipment; Wilson State Park, New York, for allowing us to photograph; and the Overlook Bike Shop in Woodstock for guidance with locations.

Thanks to Simon Wild at Raleigh UK for kindly loaning a Diamond Back mountain bike, Raleigh road bike, and an mtrax hybrid bike, as well as helmets, shoes, and pedals. Thanks to Jim McFarlane of Endura for kindly supplying clothing.

A very special thank you to Heather Kahl and her family for not only being such welcoming and generous hosts, but for suggesting the picturesque lakes, parks, woodlands, and roads near their home in New Jersey as the perfect backdrops to photograph the pictures for this book.

Finally, thanks to Jennifer Williams and Nichole Morford for invaluable editorial assistance, and to Susan Miller for the index.

PICTURE CREDITS

Additional photography by Gerard Brown. All other images copyright Dorling Kindersley.

ABOUT THE AUTHOR

Chris Sidwells is an author, journalist, and broadcaster who has written extensively about bicycles and cycling. His first book, *Mr. Tom*, was a biography of his uncle, Tom Simpson, the famous English cyclist who tragically died in the Tour de France in 1967. Chris is the author of the *Complete Bike Book* and the *Bicycle Repair Manual*, both successful titles published by Dorling Kindersley and translated into many different languages. He is a regular contributor to the two top English language cycling titles, *Cycling Weekly* and *Cycle Sport*. He has also presented programs on cycling for the BBC.

Chris is passionate about the sport and pastime of cycling, and in his writing he tries to get as many people to share that passion as he can. He has competed in every kind of bike race, from track to triathlon, and sees those who take part in the different aspects of the sport, whether touring on their bikes, using them for transport, or just riding them for the sheer pleasure of it, as all part of one big worldwide family of cyclists.

Chris splits his time between working in Europe on races such as the Tour de France, and living with his wife, two dogs, and two cats in Devon. But wherever he is, at home or abroad, his bike goes with him.